Dear Diary . . .

Dear Diary...

SOME STUDIES IN SELF-INTEREST

BY

BRIAN DOBBS

ELM TREE BOOKS

HAMISH HAMILTON · LONDON

First published in Great Britain 1974
by Elm Tree Books Ltd
90 Great Russell Street, London, WC1

Copyright © 1974 by Brian Dobbs

SBN 241 89030 6

Printed in Great Britain by
Ebenezer Baylis and Son Limited
The Trinity Press, Worcester, and London

Contents

Acknowledgements

The author and publishers wish to express their thanks to Mrs Dorothy Cheston Bennett for permission to quote from *The Journals of Arnold Bennett*, edited by Newman Flower and published by Cassell and Company Ltd.; The Bodley Head for permission to quote from Henry Williamson's *Goodbye, West Country*; Jonathan Cape Ltd. for permission to quote from *The Cecil King Diary 1965–1970*; Chatto and Windus Ltd. for permission to quote from *The Diaries of Marie Belloc Lowndes 1911–1947*, edited by Susan Lowndes; Collins Publishers for permission to quote from Harold Nicolson's *Diaries and Letters*; the Literary Estate of Virginia Woolf and the Hogarth Press for permission to quote from *A Writer's Diary*, edited by Leonard Woolf; Hutchinson Publishing Group for permission to quote from *Lloyd George: A Diary* by Francis Stevenson, edited by A. J. P. Taylor, and *Diaries 1915–1918* by Lady Cynthia Asquith; Cecil Lewis and Peter Davies Ltd. for permission to quote from *Self-Portrait: the Letters and Journals of Charles Ricketts*, edited by Cecil Lewis; The London School of Economics and Political Science for permission to quote from *Beatrice Webb's Diaries*, edited by Margaret Cole and published by the Longman Group Ltd.; Methuen and Co. Ltd. for permission to quote from *English Diaries* by Arthur Ponsonby; John Murray (Publishers) Ltd. for permission to quote from *The Diary of Lady Frederick Cavendish*, edited by John Bailey; The Society of Authors as the literary representative of the Estate of Katherine Mansfield for permission to quote from *The Journal of Katherine Mansfield*, edited by John Middleton Murry and published by Constable and Co. Ltd.; the

Acknowledgements

Editor of *The Times Literary Supplement* for permission to quote from an article by George Mikes in that periodical; and George Weidenfeld and Nicolson Ltd. for permission to quote from *Chips: the Diaries of Sir Henry Channon*, edited by Robert Rhodes James.

ONE

The Quality of the Witness

In 1922, when Baron Ponsonby wrote the first of a number of his books on diaries, he started his text with an introduction to diary writing. In it he felt able to say quite confidently that there is a very clear distinction between diary writing and other forms of writing.

> Diary writing is within the reach of every human being who can put pen to paper and no-one is in a more advantageous position than anyone else for keeping a diary. People of all ages and degrees who may never have ventured to write a line for publication and may be quite incapable of any literary effort, are able to keep a diary the value of which need not in any way suffer from their literary incapacity. On the contrary, literary talent may be a barrier to complete sincerity. Diaries may or may not be called literature; some undoubtedly have literary value, but this has nothing whatever to do with their merit as diaries.

This is a very attractive and democratic idea. Certainly it would be a tragedy if anyone were deterred from keeping a diary by the thought that he is unable to produce prose stylish enough to justify publication later or to reach a wide audience. The notion that only the high and mighty are the ones whose lives should be recorded for posterity has already blighted our knowledge of history to a shameful degree. Only within our own times has the false idea that history is only about kings and queens finally begun to be nailed for the lie it is. There is admittedly the difficulty of literacy: if a man is unable even to write his own name, he is unlikely ever to come to the attention of later generations, except by a freak. If he can leave written records, then there is always a chance that his individuality will be made known to someone beyond his own ken by virtue of space or time, and he will have made an impression, no matter how tiny, on future generations.

If Time is truly the great healer, it is also truly the great injector of interest. Its passing makes some factors of crucial contemporary import seem deadly dull (who but the trained historian or specialist now wishes to know Gladstone's attitude on the Chinese Labour question?), yet it makes others of riveting fascination. Let me put it this way. What would one do with a boxful of odd socks? Burn them? Dump them? Bury them perhaps? Yes, but what would one do if one found a boxful of odd socks, or their equivalent, dating from the sixteenth century? Put them in a glass case, of course, and charge all who wish to see them good money. The passing of time has given them a scarcity value that they did not originally possess.

On this particular point, I think the Baron is on strong ground. Due to their scarcity value, diaries written by obscure men of the past can have a real value. We can forgive faults of style, of grammar, even pomposities and boasts if, when it comes down to essentials, the diarist tells us something we did not know already. The scarcity value, however, is not to be forgotten. The diarist, though he may be turgid and verbose, has our attention so long as he is in a monopoly position. Even if he is insincere, we are still inclined to read him.

But suppose another diary of the same kind, period or specialist interest is found: what happens then? Well, we immediately begin to apply the same sort of criteria we would apply to differentiate between any two works of art – insofar as two works of art can ever be compared. We assess the relative merits of their capacity to entertain, to move, to inform, to make our life richer than it was before, in however marginal a way. We then take the superior product. In other words, we would use normal critical judgments, as we would to assess any other kind of literature.

When Baron Ponsonby lays stress on the sincerity of a diary, one can go part of the way with him. Once we suspect that an author is being dishonest with us or with himself, which I would term 'insincerity' in this context, we lose respect for him and for his art.

If we turn back to the eleventh, and best, edition of the *Encyclopedia Britannica* and refer to the entry on diaries, we will find another rule laid down for the potential diarist as a *sine qua non* for his sincerity:

> It will be perceived that, without exception, these works [i.e. Pepys's, Evelyn's and some other classic diaries] were posthumously published, and the whole conception of the diary has been that it should be for the writer alone, or, if for the public, for the public when all prejudice shall have passed away and all passion cooled down. Thus, and only thus, can the diary be written so as to impress upon its eventual readers a sense of its author's perfect sincerity and courage . . .

By putting these two qualifications together perhaps we can find an attribute which will enable us to recognize a good or even a great diary. If the diary is totally sincere and is not written for an audience within the diarist's lifetime, then we should have a good diary. If only life were that simple . . .

To examine the first half of the qualification first: no census has ever been carried out, and by the nature of things never will be, but one suspects that if the bad works of art in every form – paintings, books, symphonies, plays, etc. – were separated into two piles, one labelled 'insincere' (carried out for the money or prestige alone), the other 'sincere' (executed with burning zeal and heart-felt compulsion), the two piles would be roughly equal. In fact, if there were a measurable difference, one suspects the sincere pile would be rather higher. It is infinitely sad but true that over the country at any given moment there will be thousands of people daubing canvasses, tapping typewriters, learning lines, constructing perfect reproductions of Nelson's column from matchsticks, or writing sonnets to commemorate the appearance of the first plastic gnome of the season. And if you were to question their sincerity in carrying out any of these creative arts, they would be rightly furious at the insult. Their sincerity has never been in question for a moment; it is just that anyone with a developed critical faculty is bound to question their taste. It is still sometimes said, usually when one professional critic or other is under fire, that any man's opinion is as good as any other's. Unfortunately, it is not true. The opinion of someone steeped in the history and language, language in its broadest sense, of an art form is more likely to be of interest and value than someone who comes to that form for the first time. There is always the possibility that an unspoiled innocent of a spectator will point to the absence of the emperor's clothes, but normally we can rely on the professional tailor and cutter for an accurate sartorial assessment.

The concept that one man's diary is as good as the next's, I also beg leave to doubt. Whatever the psalm says to the contrary, out of the mouths of babes and sucklings the most common sound to be heard is a mundane cry to be fed – very necessary and very useful but not one which makes for good listening. It is true that from time to time the voice of the innocent will produce something of lasting value. It is just that for every Henri Rousseau and Grandma Moses, there are a million Sunday painters whose achievements are as low as their ambitions.

Writing in 1913 in *The Autobiography*, Anna Robeson Burr, who made more than one specialist study of autobiographical books and confessions, said this, which to me is the crux of the matter: 'the whole value of personal testimony lies in the quality of the witness.'

In other words it is not necessarily so, but the better the

writer, the more likely it is that he will be able to put his thoughts about life, other people and himself in order, and set them down on paper in a coherent fashion. The better he is at separating the spurious from the genuine, the more interesting will be the diary. The three individuals to whom I have devoted separate chapters, Evelyn, Pepys and Boswell, may all seem to ramble and be easily sidetracked. Their mood changes abruptly sometimes from gloom to euphoria. Sometimes the story they are telling emerges piecemeal because they only get the story themselves in dribs and drabs in a less than orderly fashion, so that reading their accounts is sometimes akin to opening a book at page 200 and working backwards. Different as they are in time, temperament and intention they have one thing in common, a quality all good diarists share to greater or lesser degree: they are all good witnesses and consequently their testimony is good.

What we gain from the diary form, once the diarist's hand has written and moved on, are the emotions and events of a particular day captured very soon after they have been experienced. He cannot reconsider his entry when the immediacy of the moment has receded from the memory, unless he edits it at a later date. The view may be partial, but it is the best he or she had at the time.

This is why we have no right to demand of a diary that it should present a picture of life in the round. Its focus must be, by the nature of things, the writer's immediate present. There can be no question of finding a unity of purpose over a span of months, years or lives. We cannot even ask that the diarist should have a long-term sense of proportion. That can only come in the art of biography or autobiography when the wheat can be separated from the chaff in the light of experience. (If this facet be taken as a tribute to the editors of many published diaries, where millions of sometimes boring words have been discreetly reduced to a riveting book, credit would have been given where due, and moreover where all too rarely received.) It is reasonable

though to ask that the diarist has a sense of proportion
operating on a daily basis. Ernest Hemingway was once
asked what facet a writer needed above all else. His reply was
impolite but truthful – 'a built-in shock-proof shit detector'.
He could have added that anyone who intended to keep a
diary of more than personal interest needed such a device
firing on all cylinders. It is the first quality of a good
witness.

Good witnesses are rare enough, great ones an even rarer
breed. The power of detachment, the ability of an artist to
divide himself into two separate beings, one to participate
and one to watch himself participating, while retaining an
artist's objectivity, is given to few. And it is only those few,
like Pepys and Boswell, whose diaries deserve to be published *in toto*. Their diaries, even allowing for the disadvan-
tages of the diffuse nature of the genre, have achieved the
status of great literature. Of precious few diaries can that be
said.

If the diary form then is unlikely to qualify for our attention as literature, is it worth our attention at all? There are
some who would say that it is not. In *The Times Literary
Supplement* in June 1973, the humorist George Mikes took
temporary charge of the 'Viewpoint' column and, prompted
by a reading of the serialization of Evelyn Waugh's diary in
a Sunday newspaper (my own view of Waugh's diaries will
be found on pages 111–13), directed a broadside at the *genre*.
'Diaries are a gigantic fraud', he started; and after poking
some legitimate fun at the diarist's licence to name names,
i.e. to libel and ridicule contemporaries with impunity; and
equally to drop names, i.e. to record meetings with the
famous and to ignore the existence of 'people on PAYE',
he continued:

> The truth is that the diary, as such, is a basically and
> essentially misleading and dishonest way of writing. It
> gives the impression of being intimate, of revealing one's
> innermost thoughts and closely guarded secrets. The

reader has the impression of being allowed to catch a glimpse of a secret world, a hidden sanctuary. He is allowed nothing of the sort. All the diaries of public men – writers, other artists, politicians – are written with future publication in mind. The revelations are not revelations at all but calculated plants, carefully worded messages. Historians have often remarked that we are incredibly lucky having found so many diaries kept by eighteenth-century statesmen and thus gaining an insight into their secrets, their motives, their hopes and fears. But he who lies in public will also lie in private. Those politicians knew perfectly well that their diaries would be found and used as sources. Their revelations were clever and at that time novel ways of pleading their cases.

There is much in what he says. The diary as propaganda for future generations is common enough, but he is too sweeping by far. Pepys was a public man, yet one would hesitate to dismiss his diary as a carefully written plant. We are back to our previous qualification, the quality of the witness. Good witnesses do not give testimony which is really intended only as a carefully worded message to future generations. Mikes's point about eighteenth-century states-men's diaries does not stand close examination either. The most famous of the category, the one kept by George Bubb Dodington, has been devoured by historians ever since its original publication, not for what Dodington tells us directly but what he gives away indirectly. He *did* write it to justify himself (under the terms of his will he requested his nephew to publish only those parts that would 'do honour to his memory'), but we read it because his justification gives such valuable evidence of conduct that could not be justi-fied! It is not a matter of Dodington's diary deceiving us, but of Dodington's diary giving him away to history. (If he had had any sense he would have disinherited the nephew, burned the diary, and faded thankfully into obscurity.)

For Marie Bashkirtsev, the diary had an even more

specific purpose than for Bubb Dodington. Of her own she wrote:

> If I should not live long enough to become famous, this journal will be interesting to psychologists. The record of a woman's life, written down day by day, without any attempt at concealment, as if no-one in the world were to read it, yet with the purpose of being read . . .

I think there is a contributory reason to be gleaned here of the continuing fascination of diaries. It has two facets, one for the diarist and one for the reader.

For the diarist himself or herself, the journal fundamentally arises out of a desire to capture a moment or a day of time which would otherwise be lost; lost to the diarist in later life, and to posterity after his or her death. Lacking, as nearly all of us do, the capacity for total recall, the diarist has his journal as an *aide mémoire* and souvenir rolled into one. The souvenir or the photograph can help us imperfectly to recall an occasion, a full diary entry enables us to relive it. Not only does the entry tell us what we did, it tells us how we felt about the action.

And there is another powerful factor. We all know deep in our hearts that we are on a remorseless conveyor belt carrying us, hopefully at a slow rate, from the cradle to the grave. There are occasions when the temptation to make some sort of unique record, to impose something of ourselves upon an apparently heedless world before we are gone for ever, is irresistible. Secretly, we all feel we have something unique to contribute – and deep disturbances in the psyche can occur if we are not able to feel that – but sometimes it is necessary to convince others too. The great paradox of suicide is that it is most commonly a desperate plea to live and to be appreciated to the full. It cannot be a coincidence that the more hopeless the environment and the worse the prospects of life, the more likely there is to be vandalism and a rash of graffiti. New York, for example, has what seems to be every available surface covered with aerosol arabesques and symbols – symptoms, surely, of a need to make an individual mark on unseeing and uncaring surroundings.

The diary as therapy then, or the diary as the literate man's graffiti? Up to a point yes, but even here the quality of the testimony is going to depend on the quality of the witness – graffiti by Rembrandt or Matisse would certainly be of greater interest than most – but we have now to consider the second facet, that of the reader. Even if we have proved the value of the diary for the diarist, can we prove its value for the reader?

I think we can, for so long as life itself is interesting, then other people's diaries will be. Who can resist the temptation of peeping into other people's windows when walking down a strange street at dusk when the living-room lights are on but the curtains not drawn? Reading a diary is like looking through a window at someone else's life. Admittedly the diarist can pull down the blind at any time, or at least draw the net curtains of selectivity, but even from a brief glimpse we can know more about him than we would from another's description, no matter how graphic. The diary has this documentary quality to it. We know that we are hearing the free expression of opinion in the diarist's own voice, as surely as if a microphone were recording his words. Of course, insincerity can creep in, for the perfectly honest man, whether speaker or writer, has yet to exist, but within the limitations imposed by the fact that we are dealing with human beings, we are more likely to get an honest statement in his diary than elsewhere.

The diaries of the past are unique windows on history, for when the diarist lets us peep at all, he cannot completely control what we will see in his room. He may brush all the fluff under the carpet and out of sight, but we will see the dust on the window-sill. Even more important, although the diarist will be concerned to show himself to us in the best light, fundamentally he *does* want us to look. He also wants us to see the things his contemporaries may have missed – to his disappointment, annoyance, or disgust.

It may be that there are diarists who record for themselves alone, and who destroy their diaries or arrange to have them destroyed on their death. In such cases, one can accept that the writers were sincerely concerned to keep their diaries secret. Their diaries served the same purpose as a pile of old love-letters tied up in ribbon – though time passed and the world changed, an experience of personal import had not been merely pushed into oblivion with the rest of the trivia of everyday living. Instead it could be recalled and savoured. Lord Shaftesbury would have understood this for, according to him, everyone who begins to keep a journal regrets that he did not do so before.

But if those letters, and even more so the diary, are not destroyed, then we can hazard that it was for posterity and for belated recognition that they were kept in the first place. So strong may this motive become that some diarists, in a fire, an air raid or a shipwreck, would probably choose to save their diaries before the women and children. In such cases it is not that the diarist wishes us to know that it rained on his forty-fifth birthday, but he does wish us to know that it was *his* forty-fifth birthday that was spoiled by rain.

When, later in this book, we take a look at some individual diarists and diaries of three previous centuries, the seventeenth, eighteenth and nineteenth, we will see that many of them were produced by people with no claim to fame other than their diaries. In particular, one can point to two country diaries, one by the Reverend Woodforde in the eighteenth century, and one by the Reverend Kilvert in the nineteenth. Neither man would be in the least familiar to us today if it had not been for the fact he kept a journal. Theirs are authentic voices telling us what it was like to be alive in their times and places. They offer something unique – the rarity value of the monopolist's position – and we respond gratefully. It would be a tragedy if people as yet unknown in our own times were not allowed to speak to the future with the same variety of colour and flavour. Frankly, there is some danger that they will not.

There is the danger that urban man (and even those of us who do not live in towns tend to be wholly dependent upon one) will be too absorbed by the increased flurry of daily existence to contemplate the keeping of a diary. This is not too grave a danger, for so long as men are born with the diarist's itch to record and the need to place their experiences and emotions in the deep-freeze of the diary for future consumption, diaries will continue to be kept. There is, however, another graver danger.

Sir Arthur Ponsonby's first book on diaries was published in 1922. The half century since that time has brought changes and developments that Man, *circa* 1922, would find amazing, among them, surely, the development of nation-wide radio and television. The beneficial roles of these media in increasing general awareness is incalculable. Whereas the majority of the working population in the early 1920s knew only its own community and its conventions, now the habits, thoughts and speech of a wide spectrum of people bombards the contemporary equivalent nightly in its living-room. We cannot yet be sure what effect this will have, but if it tends, as I suspect it may, to increase uniformity of thought and expression, it will be such small areas of life as the diary or the folk-song, where richness is a reflection of the rich variety of people themselves, that will be the first to be submerged by admass. When the Orkney islander, the Liverpudlian and the Cockney all think and sound alike, we will all be spiritually dead and the diary with us. Long may such a day be postponed.

It remains to explain the scheme of this book. The reader will find more attention has been given to the important issues of life – sex, religion, politics, and the like – than to the marginal. That it is sometimes thought necessary to exclude these important matters from polite conversation is what makes polite conversation tedious on occasion.

However, what we may endure and indeed demand for ten minutes' social intercourse is insufficiently rich to last us through 250 closely-written pages of a publishable diary. Diaries which have not been published are of such limited accessibility that they have automatically been excluded. So, owing to limited time and space, are diaries not available in Britain. American diaries and especially French diaries would justify volumes to themselves, but the reason for their omission is practical, not jingoistic.

From the thousands of printed diaries, those discussed here are but a random sample; someone else could make a totally different selection which would be equally valid. Similarly, someone who took an identical selection could be totally at odds with the tentative conclusions reached here. In such matters there are no absolutes, only shades of opinion. I only hope that any reader who agrees or disagrees with mine will be encouraged to read or re-read the diaries for himself.

Diaries, because they are such good reflectors of the diversity of life, wear labels or enter categories uneasily. For the convenience of discussion only, they have been divided here into religious diaries (Chapter Two), social diaries (Chapter Six), country diaries (Chapter Seven), literary diaries (Chapter Eight), political diaries (Chapter Nine), and women's diaries (Chapter Ten). In addition, Chapters Three, Four and Five are devoted to three men to whom I would give the accolade of supreme diarists. Inevitably, many diaries could be placed in more than one category. Should Caroline Fox's journal, for example, be considered as a social diary, a literary diary, or a woman's diary? In such a case, I have placed the diary where I think its interest mainly lies, but such a placing is not meant to suggest that any of the works can be formally labelled according to genus and species. If there's 'nowt so queer as folk', folk's diaries run them pretty close.

The whole development of Western man being bound up with the history of the Christian religion in its broadest sense, some brief thoughts on the development of the diary form will be found in the chapter on religious diaries. Other than in rudimentary form – the slight expansions on account books, public engagement books, uncomfortable and stilted religious confessions and the like – the diary can be said to begin in England only in the first half of the seventeenth century. It would not be true to say, however, that the diary instinct was not thought of before then, if only in rudimentary form. I am indebted to P. A. Spalding's short book *Self-Harvest*, which contains some interesting thoughts on the diary form, for a reference to Charles Plummer's address to the British Academy published in 1926. Plummer's researches into the manuscripts once kept in Irish libraries revealed an interesting phenomenon.

Before the invention of printing types, the only books in existence were those copied in manuscript from the original source. Only those with considerable wealth were able to possess libraries, but of those, both private patrons and ecclesiastical institutions employed scribes to do the copying for them. When certain Irish scribes actually laid hands on pen and parchment, they apparently considered that the main body of the text might belong to the patron, but the margins were theirs. Consequently, some medieval and later Irish manuscripts have in their margins, written in Gaelic, what one can only describe as rudimentary diary entries.

The phlegm is upon me like a mighty river, and my breathing is laboured . . . Alas, my chest, O Holy Virgin. I am Eugene O'Shiell, the scabby who wrote this . . .
May God forgive Edmund the putting colour on this book on the eve of Sunday . . .

Complaints are the most frequent:

William Magfindgaill wrote the above without chalk, without pumice, and with bad implements . . .
On my word it is a great torment to be keeping the Friday of the Passion on water, with the excellent wine which

there is in the house with us . . .
A curse on thee, O pen . . .

but on a Law manuscript held in the Trinity College,
Dublin there are such jottings which are as near to the keeping of a diary as one could imagine. Dated in 1350, the
scribe wrote:

> . . . in the second year after the coming of the plague to
> Ireland was this written, and I myself am full twenty-one
> years old . . . let every reader in pity recite a pater for my
> soul. It is Christmas Eve tonight . . . may this great
> plague pass by me and my friends, and restore us once
> more to joy and gladness. Amen. Pater Noster . . .

It is a distinct relief to see that twelve months later, he was
able to add:

> It is just a year tonight since I wrote the lines in the
> margin below; and, if it is God's will, may I reach the
> anniversary of this great Eve once more. Amen. Pater
> Noster.

There were no more notes. Perhaps he lived, perhaps he did
not; we cannot know.

From the obscure point in time that man first gave himself a name until the present, it is probable that he has had
an urge to leave some small part of himself behind after his
life is over. Perhaps starting with the first man to carve his
name or initials on a tree or a rock, and continuing through
the chronicles of the early Middle Ages when monks felt
they had to write down unusual events like the passing of a
comet, such a desire has been ever present. What follows is
a small selection of the way some people chose to respond
to that desire over the last three centuries.

BIBLIOGRAPHY

Baron Arthur Ponsonby: *English Diaries* (Methuen, 1923); *More English Diaries* (Methuen, 1927); *Scottish and Irish Diaries* (Methuen, 1927).

Marie Bashkirtsev: *Journal* (2 volumes), translated by Mathilde Blind (Cassell, 1890).

Anna Robeson Burr: *The Autobiography* (Houghton, Mifflin Co., 1909). *Religious Confessions and Confessants* (Houghton, Mifflin Co., 1914).

P. A. Spalding: *Self-Harvest: a study of diaries and the diarist* (Independent Press, 1949).

George Mikes: 'Viewpoint' article in *The Times Literary Supplement*, no. 3,719, 15 June, 1973.

Charles Plummer: *On the Colophons and Marginalia of Irish Scribes* ... From the Proceedings of the British Academy (London, 1926).

TWO

Voices, Sins and Angels

Considering the closeness of the relationship between the lonely experience of diary-keeping and the use of solitude to either pray to God or to examine one's own soul, it is only to be expected that religious diaries must loom large in all bibliographies of diaries, and that pious individuals play a large part in the history of autobiography. Page after page of philosophic meditation, self-analysis, devotional exercises, calls upon the Almighty, or verbatim accounts of contemporary sermons typify these volumes. Varying in quality from sanctimonious and self-righteous discourse to sincere and humble testament, religious diaries could provide all the source material a psychologist of religion or an historian of theological matters might require.

Christianity, over the centuries, has had a profound effect upon the autobiographical urge and its manifestations. The founder of Christianity himself, as Matthew Arnold pointed out, insisted that his followers as a matter of priority attend first of all to their inward thoughts and to the state of their hearts and feelings. It requires little imagination to see how close this is to the act of keeping a diary for anyone of religious persuasion. At its best, this might mean that the diary form was used for spiritual confession of the normal and representative kind, expressing the religious feelings common to many believers. At its worst, the journal might be the recipient of the most extraordinary, if not pathological, manifestations of a soul believing itself in touch with the divine, ranging from hallucinations to the hearing of heavenly voices. Religious emotion, like any other, can be sincere and distinguished, or cheap and transient, and its expression in diary form can reflect either of those extremes.

Although not a diary, St Augustine's *Confessions* represents a major stage in the history of autobiography, being arguably the first subjective autobiography. The author was concerned to be hortative and exemplary, trying by an account of his own thoughts and actions to warn or inspire his readers in turn. With the hindsight of centuries we can see how much influence on the Church and on Western man St Augustine's work has had, although it is almost a contradiction in terms to describe a book as influential when it had no imitator for some 650 years. Augustine says 'this is the fruit of my confessions, not of what I was but of what I am, that I may confess this not before Thee only, but in the ears also of believing souls of men'.

When Thomas à Kempis wrote, in 1440, *The Imitation of Christ* he was, like Arnold, echoing the words of his Saviour – 'a humble knowledge of thyself is a surer way to God than a deep search after learning' – but he was not expressing a view that would have found much favour in pre-Renaissance times. Once the idea that introspection might be valuable had started, it rapidly developed into a kind of norm in religious thought, and a norm which was given increasing force by the growth of monasticism. It cannot be emphasized enough, however, that this introspection did not mean that each man was able to work out his own salvation by developing his own self-awareness. In the centuries when mother Church had her firmest control over her children, the climate of opinion was such as to be unsympathetic to any expressions of individualism in any form.

The age was characterized rather by the elevation of the song above the singer. The great achievements in architecture or in manuscript decoration or in sculpture that we associate with the Gothic were *anonymous*. The philosophy was that every individual is but a representative of a common humanity, and differs from his neighbour only by his external actions, and particularly productions. His personal vicissitudes of fortune were of no interest, only his work. The work itself was, after all, for the greater glory of God, not for its individual creator. In this kind of intellectual climate, diaries were unthought of. It was only with the onset of the Renaissance with its revival of classical learning, and the Reformation with its concept of freedom of conscience, that religious and intellectual freedoms reached a stage sympathetic to self-expression and made it possible for a man to think of keeping a diary.

The landmark of the new consciousness is not actually a diary but a book of essays by a Frenchman. Written in the 1580s, Montaigne's *Essays* are profoundly original. He created an essay form to be used and re-used by writers who came after him, but more important for our present purpose, insofar as he developed the essay form, he turned his attention to his own character and attributes and his own preferences and prejudices, so that Montaigne is as much his own subject as anything on which he writes. Montaigne was not making a confession *pour encourager les autres*, he was looking at himself with an objectivity without precedent, and with a tolerant spirit rarely equalled since.

In England, the religious turmoil of the seventeenth century and the rise of the Puritan conscience brought a spate of true diaries in their wake. Before the seventeenth century in England, the only manifestations approaching the diary form were the marginalia we have already mentioned, plus official engagement books with the tersest of personal data added to the utilitarian and functional entries, plus confessional literature of a turgid nature.

The rise of the diary came in parallel with the rise of the Quakers.[1] This should not surprise us. Consider, for a moment, the attitudes of the Quakers and to what extent they represented a break with Christian tradition. In matters

[1] The term 'Quaker' was first used by a magistrate at Derby, arising from Fox's statements that henceforward people would 'tremble at the word of the Lord'.

spiritual, the Quakers renounced all external authority, i.e. the Church and the priesthood, in favour of the direct and inward guidance of the illuminating Spirit of God. To allow this Inner Light to work its divine purpose, they determinedly set aside ceremony, sacraments, conventions and teachers.

The Quaker philosophies spread like wildfire from about 1648 to the middle of the 1650s, arousing great hostility in the dominant Puritan sects of the day, though perhaps the period of severest persecution of them came after the Restoration. The Quaker protest was against formal religion as such, against ecclesiasticism, and against the literal interpretation of the Bible. At its worst the movement, with its general distrust of the intellect and of the values of a formal religious training, was a band-wagon on which many jumped, for without theological criteria to separate the genuine movements of the Spirit from the spurious, the movement attracted the egotistical along with the humble. At its best, it played the same sort of part within Protestantism that quietism did within Catholicism.

In his famous journal, George Fox, founder of the Society of Friends, gives us details of the sort of affirmation Quakers made:

> that Every man was enlightened by the Divine Light of Christ, and I saw it shine through all; And that they that believed in it came out of Condemnation and came to the Light of Life, and became the Children of it ... This I saw in the pure Openings of the Light, without the help of any Man, neither did I then know where to find it in the Scriptures, though afterwards, searching the Scriptures, I found it ...

Against the prevailing Puritan disbelief in immediate and instant revelation, Fox set out details of his own conversion at Lichfield. The lurid character of the experience is reflected in the prose.

> ... went by my eye over hedge and ditch till I came

within a mile of Lichfield; where in a great field, shepherds were keeping their sheep. Then was I commanded
by the Lord to pull off my shoes. I stood still for it was
winter; but the word of the Lord was like a fire in me. So
I put off my shoes and left them with the shepherds; and
the poor shepherds trembled, and were astonished. Then
I walked on about a mile, and as soon as I was got within
the city, the word of the Lord came to me again, saying:
Cry, 'Wo to the bloody city of Lichfield!' So I went up
and down the streets, crying with a loud voice. Wo to the
bloody city of Lichfield! ... As I went thus crying
through the streets, there seemed to me to be a channel
of blood running down the streets, and the market-place
appeared like a pool of blood ... afterwards I was to
understand, that in the Emperor Diocletian's time a
thousand Christians were martyr'd in Lichfield. So I was
to go, without my shoes, through the channel of their
blood, and into the pool of their blood in the market-
place, that I might raise up the memorial of the blood
of those martyrs, which had been shed above a thousand
years before, and lay cold in their streets. So the sense of
this blood was upon me, and I obeyed the word of the
Lord ...

Having been given this vision, Fox tramped the country,
with frequent interludes in prison, for the light which
brought St Augustine peace brought in Fox's case a burning
torch which it was his sacred duty to carry around the
country. In his diary, which it must be admitted was
written or dictated on a retrospective basis, one can see the
biblical influence on the imagery of the prose, and, with the
exception of Bunyan, one can think of no one else evoking
quite this kind of imagery.

Evoking it, that is, and sounding fresh and original.
After Fox, there were a hundred Quakers influenced by his
journal to keep one of their own. Unfortunately – I say
unfortunately because we are here concerned with literary

usefulness rather than proof of religious influence – those who came after Fox and imitated him were often of a poor standard of education and literacy and could do nothing but mimic his rolling phrases and testamental vocabulary at an inferior second-hand. In some cases, the simplest internal or external actions were declared to be 'divinely inspired'. To some extent this was Fox's fault. Despite his massive influence on later centuries, when Methodists, Wesleyans and Salvationists used, broadly speaking, Fox's methods to take the word of God to the people at large, Fox fell into the trap himself: certain passages betray his evident satisfaction that a misfortune befalling any of his enemies must be clear evidence of God intervening on his behalf. This is what happened to a Colonel Rouse in 1656:

> Then said I, 'If it be so, be still and receive answers from me to what thou sayest.' Then I was moved to speak the word of life to him in God's dreadful power; which came so over him that he could not open his mouth; his face swelled and was red like a turkey; his lips moved and he mumbled something; but the people thought he would have fallen down. I stepped to him and he said, 'I was never so in my life before'; for the Lord's power stopped the evil power and air in him; so that he was almost choked. The man was ever after very loving to Friends, and never so full of airy words to us, though he was full of pride; but the Lord's power came over him, and the rest that were with him.

A heckler who had the temerity to heckle at a Fox meeting in 1659 fared even worse:

> setting himself just opposite to the Friend that was speaking, he lolled his tongue out of his mouth having his bear's skin on his back, and so made sport to his wicked followers, and caused a great disturbance in the meeting. And as he returned from the meeting there was a bull-baiting in the way which he stayed to see; and coming

within the bull's reach, he struck his horn under the man's chin into his throat, and struck his tongue out of his mouth, so that it hung lolling out, as he had used it before in derision in the meeting. And the bull's horn running up into the man's head, he swung him about upon his horn. Thus he that came to do mischief amongst God's people was mischiefed himself.

A bull seems a common agent in such divine retribution for in 1663, when a Colonel Robinson (an M.P. and a magistrate who had frequently imprisoned Friends) was gored by his own animal, Fox was very pleased:

> Thus does the Lord sometimes make some examples of His just judgment upon the persecutors of His people, that others may fear and learn to beware . . .

In view of the privations suffered by Fox and his followers for their beliefs, perhaps we should forgive the occasional reluctance to turn the other cheek.

The fervour of a Fox did not extend to all clergymen by any means. For every Fox burning with zeal, there were a hundred clergymen who knew the virtues of their local flock, turning a blind eye to sins unless they were particularly difficult to ignore, giving comfort in time of family upheaval, and seeking to do good by example but not worrying day in and day out about the state of their eternal souls. And yet there were others again, convinced that they were doing the Lord's work and fretting lest a day passed without a blow struck for their beliefs.

One such was William Dowsing, 'a Parliamentary Visitor appointed under a warrant from the Earl of Manchester for demolishing the superstitious pictures and ornaments of churches etc. within the County of Suffolk in the years 1643–44'. In brief, Dowsing was a Puritan determined to rid Suffolk churches of the slightest taint of idolatry. There are iconoclasts and iconoclasts – Dowsing was something special. Not only did he go on the rampage through Suffolk churches, he kept a diary lest any window, ornament or image smashed should escape posterity's attention:

> Haverhill: *Jan the 6th 1643* We brake down about a hundred superstitious Pictures; and seven Fryars hugging a Nunn [!]; and the Picture of God and Christ; and diverse others very superstitious; and 200 had been broke down before I came. We took away two popish Inscriptions with *ora pro nobis* and we beat down a great stoneing Cross on the top of the Church . . .

A useful indication that not everyone approved of Dowsing's activities is the eye-witness who described him as one

> who goes about the Country like a Bedlam breakinge glasse windowes, having battered and beaten downe all our painted glasse, not only in our Chapels, but (contrary to Order) in our publique schooles, Colledge Halls, Libraryes, and Chambers, mistaking perhapps the liberall Arts for Saints . . .

Dowsing, who incidentally prided himself on his 'Lating' (*sic*), is, like Fox, a powerful reminder of the passions that religious controversy could raise. Other men's fervour was directed more inwardly, for example that of Dr Rutty, whose diary made Dr Johnson roar with laughter. The good Doctor clearly placed Rutty in his fourth class of egotists – 'the journalists, temporal and spiritual: Elias Ashmole, William Lilly, George Whitefield, John Wesley, and a thousand other old women and fanatick writers of memoirs and meditations . . .' Johnson's cynicism was a little misplaced. Dr Rutty (1697–1774) took up diary-writing in his mid-fifties in the naïve but rather touching belief that accounts of his own foibles might enable others to come more easily to terms with their own. It is the minor character of the sins, and the seriousness with which they were regarded by their author, that so amused Johnson:

> Rose **too** late: O the dull body!

Gripes from excess
A hypochondriac obnubilation from wind and indigestion
Too idle in bed today: O flesh, thou Clog!
Piggish at meals.

There is, however, something genuinely affecting about poor Rutty's last entry: 'The voice of God now sounds louder in my great infirmity of being scarcely able to bear the cold . . .' He died four months later, aged 77.

Another diarist, whose life almost spans the entire eighteenth century from 1703 to 1791, and who kept a diary for sixty-six years, came from Johnson's category of 'fanatick writers of memoirs and meditations'. Certainly there is something 'fanatick' about a man who can spend over fifty years tramping or riding the roads of England for hundreds of thousands of miles, delivering perhaps forty thousand sermons, and, in the opinion of Mr Lecky, the distinguished historian, saving England from a social revolution in the process. His intentions in keeping a diary were clear: 'that he might see his life in black and white and so be in a position to judge accurately as to his own motives, attainments, doings and failures . . .' The traveller and diarist was of course John Wesley, and his diary has been called (by Augustine Birrell) 'the most amazing record of human exertion ever penned or endured'. Under nine stone and but three inches over five feet in height, Wesley was said by many of his contemporaries to be an attractive and witty personality. Even Johnson conceded that he could talk well on any subject, and Scott pays tribute to the excellence of his anecdotes. It is, however, as if so frail a frame could not have achieved so much if he had permitted himself a moment of relaxation. Consequently, Wesley's diary tends to be a bit forbidding, the record of a man with unwavering devotion to duty, and an unquenchable appetite for work, but one who forgot sometimes to smile rather than chastise.

His father was an Epworth clergyman, though it was his

mother who brought him and her other eighteen children
up in the truths of the Christian faith. John was sent to
Charterhouse and thence to Christ Church, Oxford, in
1720. He stayed there for five years until ordained as a
deacon. His reading was formidably theological and he was
particularly influenced by a grimly titled tome *The Rules for
Holy Living and Dying*, by which, he records:

> I was exceedingly affected with that part in particular
> which relates to purity of intention. Instantly, I resolved
> to dedicate all my life to God: all my thoughts, and words
> and actions.

For the next thirteen years, this exceptionally serious
young man was to seek his own salvation by prayer, meditation and self-analysis. He became a Fellow at Lincoln
College, Oxford where he was the unofficial leader of a
group of Bible readers which included his own brother
Charles. As he and his colleagues were spectacularly punc-
tilious in taking Holy Communion, the undergraduates
dubbed them 'Bible Moths' and 'Methodists'. (The latter,
like the term 'Quaker', was an epithet meant to be derisive
but which actually outlived its coiners.) I think it of some
importance that at this stage Wesley seemed to be concerned primarily with his own salvation, rather than with
the conversion of others.

He failed to get his father's old living at Epworth, and in
1735 he was invited to minister the Christian needs of the
European community in Georgia. After an eventful Atlantic
crossing when a storm frightened Wesley but not the
Moravians on board (Wesley later put this down to his own
lack of faith compared with them), he arrived in the United
States.

The Georgian ministry was not the happiest or smoothest
interlude in his life. From the start there was friction.
Wesley was a firm believer in his mission to minister to the
spiritual needs of the Georgian Indians. The local white
community were equally strong in their belief that he was

2

there to administer theirs. The friction was compounded when Wesley fell in love with the niece of Savannah's chief magistrate. She married a Mr Williamson instead, but when Wesley refused her communion on the basis of her 'unworthiness', his enemies inevitably took the view that it was jealousy on his part, rather than sin on hers, which had led to so drastic a step. Her uncle sued Wesley for defamation, but Wesley neatly side-stepped the action by claiming that civil courts had no authority to judge matters ecclesiastical. The result was a stalemate, but it brought the Georgia mission to an end.

One would have to read between the lines of the Georgia section of the diary to glean an accurate picture of the affair, but of the most important event in Wesley's life in May 1738 we are given full details. We have space here only for extracts:

> *May 24th, 1738* In the evening I went very unwillingly to a society in Aldersgate St where one was reading Luther's preface to the Romans. About a quarter to nine, while he was describing the change which God works in the heart through faith in Christ, I felt my heart strangely warmed. I felt I did trust in Christ, Christ alone for salvation: and an assurance was given me that He had taken away *my* sins, even *mine*, and save *me* from the law of sin and death . . .
>
> *May 25th* The moment I awaked, 'Jesus Master' was in my heart and in my mouth; and I found all my strength lay in keeping my eye fixed upon Him, and my soul waiting on Him continually . . .

From 1738 onwards, this renewed faith and zeal sent him on his great offensive – Wesley the scholar became Wesley the Evangelist, anxious above all else to spread the gospel throughout the length and breadth of the country. Overriding the social details we can glean from the account of his travels is this drive onwards never wavering from its purpose for half a century. Even his recipe for good health would be more likely to kill than cure in most cases; it stemmed from

1. My constantly rising at four for about fifty years.
2. My generally preaching at five in the morning; one of the most healthy exercises in the world.
3. My never travelling less, by sea and land, than four thousand five hundred miles in a year.

And this from a man in his eighties! – although one does wonder who got up in time to *hear* sermons preached at 5 a.m. Only towards the end do his incredible physical powers begin to fade:

> I am now an old man, decayed from head to foot. My eyes are dim; my right hand shakes much; my mouth is hot and dry every morning; I have a lingering fever almost every day; my motion is weak and slow . . .

but even then he has little time to dwell on these novel infirmities for, he adds: 'However, blessed be God, I do not slack my labour; I can preach and write still . . .'

While the zealous Wesley continued to tramp the country, other clergymen stayed put. The Reverend William Jones, who left his home in Abergavenny to become the curate and vicar of Broxbourne from 1781 to 1821, was one of them. He was influenced at second hand by Wesley, particularly in the matter of keeping a journal. One of Wesley's disciples at Lincoln College, the Reverend James Hervey, a devotional writer of some note during his own time, urged his readers to keep diaries. It was not posterity's but the diarist's own good that he had in mind:

> Compile a secret History of your Heart & Conduct. Take notice of the manner in which your Time is spent, & of the strain which runs through your Discourse . . . Minute down your sins of Omission. Observe the frame of your spirit in religious Duties, with what reluctance they are undertaken, with what indevotion performed; with how

many wanderings of thought, & how much dulness of desire. Register those secret Faults, to which none but the all-seeing Eye discerns. Often contemplate yourself in this faithful Mirror . . .

The Reverend Jones took the advice of his mentor very much to heart for not only did he keep a diary, he also kept a Book of Domestic Lamentations for the cataloguing of matrimonial and household difficulties. I have quoted Hervey's advice, however, because it captures one of the most common reasons for the keeping of religious diaries. The habit may indeed have led to a great number of sin-free Christian lives, but it certainly produced hundreds of inferior diaries, for the spirit of self-condemnation and morbid searchings-out of sin is antithetical to making for good reading.

The Reverend Jones's leitmotif throughout the three thousand pages of his diary (of which, of course, only a fraction has been printed) are Rutty-like complaints of failures to preserve a spotless soul – 'Vilest of the Vile' and 'Monster of Iniquity' are his commonest self-appellations. His diary would not be worth reading if this were all, but he is self-revealing in other less self-conscious ways. He is sufficiently narrow-minded to disapprove of chess on Sundays, and rejoices when an acquaintance gives up swearing, yet when he spends two years in Jamaica, it seems that although the social evil of slave-flogging disgusts him ('How disgraceful to Christianity are those professors of it who imagine poor oppressed negroes to be formed *by nature* for no other end than the exercise of their cruelty and the gratification of their brutish lusts . . .'), it cannot stir him to speak out against the practice:

Were I to say to these brutal Ruffians and Murderers of Negroes what I write of them, I'm sure the least harsh term they would think I deserved would be 'a henhearted simpleton' or 'a damned fool'!

That others might not want to hear their opinions would

never have deterred a Fox or a Wesley from speaking out.

The most entertaining aspect of Jones's diary is that the same reluctance to speak out evidently manifested itself in his relationship with his wife. Some of the entries he censored himself by tearing out the pages (the passages covering his period of courtship and marriage of Theodoria Jessopp in 1781, for example), but some remain to delight us. 'May we be blessed . . . & happy, for ever happy, in each other!', he prays in 1782, and his wife clearly came up to expectations, for he writes in 1783, 'A better [wife], one more calculated to make my life comfortable and happy, I firmly believe Heaven could not have given me'. But as the years pass, it seems, 'My wife & I . . . seem to be disputing about the mastery'. If so, he was clearly the loser, concluding with exasperation, 'I am no match for her High Mightiness . . .'.

These rather charming human touches do much to lighten the Jones diary, but the diary kept by Richard Hurrell Froude, the distinguished but short-lived Tractarian whose last years coincided with the start of the Oxford Movement, carries no such redeeming features. Adopting the Hervey doctrine with a vengeance, he too has a Rutty-like horror of gluttony. Prompted to keep a diary by reading his mother's, he writes as if his condemnation to hell-fire was automatic if the slightest lapse from perfection went unrecorded.

I am in a most conceited way besides being very ill-tempered and irritable . . . Disgusting self-complacent thoughts have kept continually obtruding themselves upon me on the score of my paltry abstinences. What I give up costs me no great effort . . . Was disgustingly ostentatious at dinner in asking for a china plate directly as I had finished my meat . . . what I ate was of the plainest sort and I took no variety yet even this was partly the effect of accident and I certainly rather exceeded in quantity as I was muzzy and sleepy after dinner . . .

Froude was only thirty-three when he died in 1836, but how naturally Victorian he seems in showing so morbid an inner life obsessed by the concept of sin in any shape or form. Did he have any doubts at all, one wonders, when he re-read his diary and concluded, 'I can hardly identify myself with the person it describes'. It is a verdict the modern reader is likely to share.

No such self-doubts plague the writing in *Diary Earthly and Spiritual,* a publication which saw the light of day in the 1890s as a tribute to its keeper James Johnston. For Mr Johnston, the religious life was packed with certainties; certainties that if no one else ever saw his nocturnal companions, that did not mean that they did not exist. It was his bounden duty moreover to tell the rest of us about them. Mr Johnston was in the unique position of being the only man able to get in touch with angels and with the old-time prophets. A golden age angel expressed regret that James was the only man present at this union between earth and heaven, but it was no less a figure than Abraham who set the angel's mind at rest by explaining that James would be a witness of the proceedings for the rest of mankind. He describes the scene:

> I was introduced by Abraham and when seated on my right were twelve angels from the Golden Age; more towards the front, and on my right were a like number from the Silver Age, and so on of the other two ages. This half-circle was completed by ten angels from the late-found world. These, of course, were towards my left hand . . .

Of course.

At times, Mr Johnston's semi must have been severely over-crowded. Sometimes, the visitors were modest in numbers: '*December 21st* Abraham and David say, that . . . there are four angel Princes who are coming to see me shortly . . .' Four angel princes were no problem (they turned up as promised at 3 a.m. on the morning of 24

December), but how he coped with his other guests must remain a mystery, for at various times he was descended upon by 146 Gentoos, 100 Hindoos, 200 Africans and 100 Ethiopians, and 120 strangers from Greece, Italy, and North and South America.

And contrary to the common belief that the non-conformist chapels were of civilizing influence among the Celtic races, Mr Johnston knew different, for on 23 May he was visited by '48 savages, native inhabitants of South Wales . . .'.

We must now reluctantly leave Mr Johnston with his visions while we examine the secular diary in some of its many aspects, starting with three men who in quite different ways, brought the form to a kind of perfection.

BIBLIOGRAPHY

The Journal of George Fox, first published 1694. Revised edition by Norman Penny in Everyman Library (Dent), 1962.

William Dowsing: *The Journal of William Dowsing*, first published 1786. New edition with notes by C. H. E. White (Parsey and Hayes, Ipswich, 1885).

John Rutty: *A Spiritual Diary and Soliloquies*, first published in 2 volumes in London in 1776. A number of later editions.

John Wesley: *The Journal of the Reverend John Wesley*, first published in 4 volumes in 1827. An enlarged edition in 8 volumes edited by Nehemiah Curnock and published by Robert Culley in London, 1909–16. A number of later editions.

Reverend William Jones: *The Diary of the Reverend William Jones*, edited by O. F. Christie (Brentano's, London, 1929).

Richard Hurrell Froude: *The Remains of the late Reverend Richard Hurrell Froude*, edited by J. H. Newman and J. Keble (Rivington, London and Derby, 1839).

James Johnston: *Diary Spiritual and Earthly of James Johnston* (Richard Clay and Sons, London, 1910).

THREE

The Eye Witness

For some men and women, the main subject of their diaries is unquestionably themselves. Of those who, on the other hand, seem to have an insatiable curiosity about the world around them, and an irresistible urge to set down in their journals their reactions to external rather than internal events, John Evelyn has held a special place for over 150 years. The diaries he kept for an extraordinary sixty-five years from 1641 to 1706 – his own life spanned from 1620 to 1706 – have thrilled historians ever since their original discovery and publication in 1818.

It is easy to see why. Evelyn supplies a concise detailed narrative of his times which aims at verisimilitude and precision; when he travels to France, Italy or Holland, the story of his journeys are a mine of information; when he stays at home, we can glean from his pages an invaluable picture of life under the last representatives of the Stuart family upon the throne of England, and under William III; and through his eyes we see seventeenth-century England, an England at peace and at civil war, an England veering from austerity to dissipation, from frivolity to deep seriousness.

Evelyn the public recording angel can never, however, quite suppress Evelyn the man with an insatiable nose for the phenomena of the natural world and an eye for the man-made beauties within it. All of us at home or on our travels notice a church here, a garden there, a painting on the wall, a panorama, a landscape; we stop, we look, we pass on. Evelyn stops, looks, opens his diary and records. The motives of the monarchs and politicians who controlled the destiny of Evelyn's England – and his very wide experience brought him into contact with many aspects of society – never quite arouse his curiosity and awe so much as a new discovery of contemporary craftsmanship. How things worked was a joy, how politicians worked perhaps a bit of a bore.

> *February 24th, 1655* I was showed a table-clock whose balance was only a crystal ball, sliding on parallel wires, without being at all fixed, but rolling from stage to stage till falling on a spring concealed from sight, it was thrown up to the utmost channel again, made with an imperceptible declivity, in this continual vicissitude of motion prettily entertaining the eye every half minute, and the next half giving progress to the hand that showed the hour, and giving notice by a small bell, so as in 120 half minutes, or periods of the bullet's falling on the ejaculatory spring, the clock-part struck. This very extraordinary piece (richly adorned) had been presented by some German Prince to our late King, and now in possession of the Usurper; valued at 200*l*.

This is typically Evelyn – the urge to record in detail what he has seen – and although he adds some information to give us an indication of the object's value in monetary terms, he forbears to add any judgment on its aesthetic merit at all. Naturally, his wealth of telling detail has made his diary an unparalleled source of evidence for art historians of the period, but it is very rare for him actually to add his own feeling. When he does it comes as a bit of an aside, almost delivered out of the side of his mouth accompanied by a lofty sniff. In 1645 he was in Venice and paid the obligatory visit to St Mark's:

> The church is also Gothic; yet for the preciousness of the materials, being of several rich marbles, abundance of porphyry, serpentine, &c., far exceeding any in Rome, St. Peter's hardly excepted. I much admired the splendid history of our blessed Saviour, composed all of mosaic

2*

over the *facciata*, below which and over the chief gates are cast four horses in copper as big as the life, the same that formerly were transported from Rome by Constantine to Byzantium, and thence by the Venetians hither. They are supported by eight porphyry columns, of very great size and value. Being come into the Church, you see nothing, and tread on nothing, but what is precious. The floor is all inlaid with agates, lazulis, chalcedons, jaspers, porphyries, and other rich marbles, admirable also for the work; the walls sumptuously incrusted, and presenting to the imagination the shapes of men, birds, houses, flowers, and a thousand varieties. The roof is of most excellent mosaic . . .

He continues in the same vein describing the relics, the altar, the doors, the pillars and the sculpture. I quote the passage for two reasons. Firstly, if St Mark's had ever been destroyed in the centuries of turmoil of Italian history, we would have been able to glean from Evelyn a very good picture of what the building looked like (in fact, the cast horses he describes were later taken back to Paris by Napoleon though they were sent back to Venice in 1815), and secondly, whatever the quality of the decoration, it did not save the building from his disapproval: 'After all that is said, this church is, in my opinion, much too dark and dismal.'

This is a relatively rare instance of Evelyn expressing any kind of moral or aesthetic judgment on what he has seen. More commonly we get a kind of verbal photograph and the opinions are left to us ourselves. We can enjoy his account of an elephant seen in Rotterdam in 1641:

It was a beast of a monstrous size, yet as flexible and nimble in the joints, contrary to the vulgar tradition, as could be imagined from so prodigious a bulk and strange fabric; but I most of all admired the dexterity and strength of its proboscis, on which it was able to support two or three men, and by which it took and reached whatever was offered to it; its teeth were but short, being a female, and not old ...

or his visit to the opera in Venice in 1645,

> where comedies and other plays are represented in recitative music, by the most excellent musicians, vocal and instrumental, with variety of scenes painted and contrived with no less art of perspective, and machines for flying in the air, and other wonderful notions; taken together, it is one of the most magnificent and expensive diversions the wit of man can invent.

or the ornithological wonders to be seen in St James's Park in 1665:

> I saw various animals, and examined the throat of the *Onocrotylus*, or pelican, a fowl between a stork and a swan; a melancholy water-fowl, brought from Astracan by the Russian Ambassador; it was diverting to see how he would toss up and turn a flat fish, plaice, or flounder, to get it right into his gullet at its lower beak, which, being filmy, stretches to a prodigious wideness when it devours a great fish. Here was also a small water-fowl, not bigger than a moorhen, that went almost quite erect, like the penguin of America; it would eat as much fish as its whole body weighted; I never saw so unsatiable a devourer, yet the body did not appear to swell the bigger ... The park was at this time stored with numerous flocks of several sorts of ordinary and extra-ordinary wild fowl, breeding about the Decoy, which for being near so great a city, and among such a concourse of soldiers and people, is a singular and diverting thing ...

In these and many other extracts which could be quoted, we can see what Virginia Woolf meant when she suggested that although Evelyn was no literary genius capable of producing a telling and memorable phrase to implant itself in the memory, he nevertheless wrote so well that we get 'a perceptible tingle of communication, so that without laying stress on anything in particular, stopping to dream, stopping to laugh, stopping to look, we are yet taking notice all the time'!

It is this very tingle of communication that makes the Evelyn diary so fresh and live when read by a modern reader. Coming across a gap of 300 years, we can almost hear his voice, perhaps a little pedantically precise in articulation and fussy in tone, imparting the news of some fresh phenomenon as if he were quietly retailing the weekend's gossip to acquaintances in a bar one Monday lunchtime.

What is still more extraordinary is that his urge to record does not switch off at any time. Where others might turn their heads away, or draw a discreet veil of silence over the seamier sights, Evelyn goes on watching and goes on scribbling. With the possible exception of a contemporary war photographer opening his lens and closing his heart to the horrors of the world around him, I can think of few witnesses capable of giving us such graphic and yet morally neutral pictures of, for example, a tiny incident witnessed in Genoa harbour:

> Here I could not but observe the sudden and devilish passion of a seaman, who plying us was intercepted by another fellow, that interposed his boat before him and took us in; for the tears gushing out of his eyes, he put his finger in his mouth and almost bit it off by the joint, showing it to his antagonist as an assurance to him of some bloody revenge, if ever he came near that part of the harbour again . . .

or, more seriously, when Evelyn visits Paris and files into a dungeon for all the world as if it were a stage spectacle with painted scenery and simulated action:

> *March 11th 1651* I went to the Chatelet, or prison, where a malefactor was to have the question, or torture, given

to him, he refusing to confess the robbery with which he was charged, which was thus: they first bound his wrist with a strong rope, or small cable, and one end of it to an iron ring made fast to the wall, about four feet from the floor, and then his feet with another cable, fastened about five feet farther than his utmost length to another ring on the floor of the room. Thus suspended, and yet lying but aslant, they slid a horse of wood under the rope which bound his feet, which so exceedingly stiffened it, as severed the fellow's joints in a miserable sort, drawing him out in length in an extraordinary manner, he having only a pair of linen drawers on his naked body. Then, they questioned him of a robbery (the Lieutenant being present, and a clerk that wrote), which not confessing, they put a higher horse under the rope, to increase the torture and extension. In this agony, confessing nothing, the executioner with a horn (just such as they drench horses with) stuck the end of it into his mouth, and poured the quantity of two buckets of water down his throat and over him, which so prodigiously swelled him, as would have pitied and affrighted any one to see it; for all this, he denied all that was charged to him. They then let him down, and carried him before a warm fire to bring him to himself, being now to all appearance dead with pain. What became of him, I know not ... There was another malefactor to succeed, but the spectacle was so uncomfortable, that I was not able to stay the sight of another. It represented to me the intolerable sufferings which our Blessed Saviour must needs undergo, when his body was hanging with all its weight upon the nails on the cross.

I do not think that the description of the horrific scene could have been written by someone genuinely 'pitied and affrighted'. Evelyn's only recoil from the horror seems to be based on the parallel with the Crucifixion (he was a very religious man in common with most of his fellows and many entries tell us of the sermons he heard) rather than upon any realization that the poor wretch being practically torn apart before his eyes was a fellow human being.

This is not to say that Evelyn was a cruel man: what characterizes him far more, in my view, is that in both the passages about the torture and those about the architectural wonders before him, he demonstrates that his curiosity exceeds any other emotion. Any cruelty inherent in watching and recording the torture is far exceeded by the desire to see how the matter is done – *how* the man is chained up, *how* the pressure is applied to his pathetic limbs, what *happens* when a man has two buckets of water poured inside him. The true parallel for this is surely not the sadist who gains any pleasure from the sight of a fellow in pain, but the child who uncomprehendingly pulls the wings off a fly in an attempt to find out what makes the insect buzz. It is this capacity to display the kind of eager curiosity that most of us lose on reaching maturity that seems to characterize Evelyn, and what makes his company a joy. To spend an hour with Evelyn is to see seventeenth-century England or Europe through the eyes of a child with the sense of wonder and awe evoked in a child seeing a thing for the first time.

When an electronic device in a cabinet in the corner of the living-room brings a modern child images of the exotic and the rare at the turn of a switch, it is all too easy to lose the capacity to be surprised at anything, and perhaps this is why Evelyn's evident astonishment at elephants, or the opera, which to us are commonplace, is so refreshing. We must remember however that it is only in his capacity for surprise and enthusiasm that Evelyn is in any way child-like. His contemporaries would have found him, quite correctly, one of the most sophisticated men of his time. His achievements stretched far beyond that of a secret and humble scribbler. In fact he was a man who could have fitted comfortably into the Italian Renaissance – a virtuoso with an antiquarian bent, a man with an insatiable appetite for knowledge almost regardless of its usefulness and unbounded by academic distinctions. To him, art, culture, history, science and religion were one.

He was born into the family of a wealthy English gentleman, and bred to the sense of values implied by that social setting. In short, he was an Anglican in religion and a monarchist in politics. These values or prejudices, depending on one's own point of view, came naturally to him, but they were instilled with a strong sense of toleration and liberality of sentiment. In a century when half of England was prepared to go to war to bend the other half to its own persuasion, John Evelyn was too amiable a man to wish evil even upon those who disagreed with him. Thus, when other men rose like comets under one authority only to fall as spectacularly under the next, the Evelyns of the world survived. He was an enthusiastic Royalist who thought of fighting for Charles I but wisely decided against it, and he corresponded with Charles II in exile, yet he returned to England in 1652 when the Royalist cause was lost, and had no difficulty in preserving his estates and in settling down to live happily under the Interregnum. After the Restoration he rose in court circles to become Keeper of the Privy Seal, but when James II's ill-fated attempt to catholicize England called upon him to apply the Seal to some particularly Popish documents, he took the infinitely wise precaution of disappearing temporarily until the sealing ceremonies were over. James II duly appointed a Catholic keeper to take his place in 1687, but Evelyn's discretion provoked neither James nor his Dutch successor to reprisals. For a man with such a nose, he was very expert in keeping it clean.

With the independence provided by his wealth, Evelyn could indulge in a literary career starting with the translation from the French of a work called *Of Liberty and Servitude* by La Mothe Le Vayer in 1649 and extending over the whole fields of his multifarious interests. Quaintly titled as many of his publications were, they show ample proof, if such were needed, of the breadth if not the depth of his scholarship. There was *Sculpture, or the History and Art of Chalcography and Engraving on Mezzotint* in 1662; there was *A Philosophical Discourse of Earth relating to the Culture and Improvement of it for Vegetation etc.* in 1675; *Numismata, a Discourse on Medals . . . with a Digression concerning Physiognomy* in 1697; and, the most famous in its time, *Sylva, or a Discourse of Forest Trees and the Propagation of Timber; to which is annexed Pomona, an Appendix concerning Fruit Trees in relation to Cider etc.* in 1664. These were few among many. *Sylva* (if one may so abbreviate) caused a deal of interest mainly because of the naval application of timber and its crucial role in England's defence from her enemies. Like many a promising idea, however, it went full bureaucratic circle when the Navy Office showed interest and referred it to the Royal Society, who referred it back to John Evelyn! Evelyn was, one almost wants to say naturally, a founder member of the Royal Society where he was on an equal footing with scientists like Boyle, Newton and Hooke, and where he later became Secretary (he is believed to have been offered the Presidency too but declined it). It is particularly heartening too to record for our environment-conscious age that Evelyn also worried about urban pollution to the extent of writing and publishing *Fumifugium, or the Inconveniences of the Aer and Smoak of London Dissipated, together with some Remedies humbly proposed* as early as 1661.

With this other capacity to seek scientific answers to contemporary horticultural, artistic or social problems in mind, it is only if we remember his child-like sense of discovery that we can understand either his total credulity at the manifestations of the natural world, or his capacity to turn things to his unexpected advantage:

> after we had supped, we embarked and passed that night through the Fens, where we were so pestered with those flying glow-worms, called *Luccioli*, that one who had

never heard of them, would think the country full of sparks of fire. Beating some of them down, and applying them to a book, I could read in the dark by the light they afforded.

Somehow, the idea of the Royal Fellow reading by the light of a glow-worm is irresistible, and indeed we have to remember that the state of scientific knowledge in his time cast just as little light as a glow-worm upon many aspects of the world around him. As a result, severe weather, an odd happening, an outbreak of disease, figure more largely in Evelyn's world than they do in ours. Frequently such events were looked on as evidence of divine disapproval, signs and portents of worse perhaps to come.

June 25th, 1652 After a drought of near four months, there fell so violent a tempest of hail, rain, wind, thunder, and lightning, as no man had seen the like in his age; the hail being in some places four or five inches about, brake all glass about London especially at Deptford, and more at Greenwich.

Jan 24th, 1684 The frost continuing more and more severe ... it was a severe judgement on the land, the trees not only splitting as if by lightning-struck, but men and cattle perishing in divers places, and the very seas so locked up with ice, that no vessels could stir out or come in. The fowls, fish, and birds, and all our exotic plants and greens, universally perishing ... London, by reason of the excessive coldness of the air hindering the ascent of smoke, was so filled with the fulmiginous steam of the sea-coal, that hardly could one see across the streets, and this filling the lungs with its gross particles, exceedingly obstructed the breast, so as one could scarcely breathe. Here was no water to be had from the pipes and engines, nor could the brewers and divers other tradesmen work, and every moment was full of disastrous accidents.

April 22nd, 1694 A fiery exhalation rising out of the sea, spread itself in Montgomeryshire a furlong broad, and many miles in length, burning all straw, hay, thatch, and grass, but doing no harm to trees, timber, or any solid things, only firing barns, or thatched houses. It left such a taint on the grass as to kill all the cattle that eat of it. I saw the attestations in the hands of the sufferers. It lasted many months . . .

December 29th, 1695 The small-pox increased exceedingly, and was very mortal. The Queen died of it on the 28th.

February 19th, 1699 A most furious wind, such as has not happened for many years, doing great damage to houses and trees, by the fall of which several persons were killed.

Manifestations like these were profitable breeding grounds for fears and superstitions. Death, particularly at the hands of pestilence and disease, was ever present. The average life-expectancy was low, and when the grim reaper wielded his scythe, the rich and the mighty were mown down together with the poor and the wretched. Evelyn over his long life was to know many a bereavement, that most depressing accompaniment to growing old. Some of the most moving passages in his whole diary are those recording the deaths of the children that were unexpectedly taken from him, and there is a note of nobility and dignity in his quiet resignation in the face of the tragedies.

January 27th, 1658 After six fits of a quartan ague, with which it pleased God to visit him, died my dear son, Richard, to our inexpressible grief and affliction, five years and three days old only, but at that tender age a prodigy for wit and understanding; for beauty of body, a very angel; for endowment of mind, of incredible and rare hopes . . .

He tells us at length of young Richard's accomplishments, which do indeed sound quite remarkable for a child of five. Even though it sounds as if some degree of negligence may have contributed to the death, Evelyn is not bitter:

> In my opinion, he was suffocated by the women and maids that attended him, and covered him too hot with blankets as he lay in a cradle, near an excessive hot fire in a close room . . .

Rather, he bows his head to the seemingly inevitable:

> Here ends the joy of my life, and for which I go even mourning to the grave.

Tragedy, however, had not yet finished with Evelyn. Just over a fortnight later he writes:

> *February 15th, 1658* The afflicting hand of God being still upon us, it pleased Him also to take away from us this morning my youngest Son, George, now seven weeks languishing at nurse, breeding teeth, and ending in a dropsy. God's holy will be done! He was buried in Deptford church, the 17th following.

Six years later, another son is taken from him:

> *March 26th, 1664* It pleased God to take away my son, Richard, now a month old, yet without any sickness or danger perceivably, being to all appearances a most likely child; we suspected much the nurse had over-lain him; to our extreme sorrow, being now again reduced to one: but God's will be done.

His daughter Mary, for whom he had had the greatest love since the death of little Richard, was not destined to outlive her father either:

> *March 7th, 1685* My daughter, Mary, was taken with the small-pox, and there soon was found no hope of her recovery. A great affliction to me: but God's holy will be done!
> *March 10th* She received the blessed Sacrament; after

which, disposing herself to suffer what God should determine to inflict, she bore the remainder of her sickness, with an extraordinary patience and piety, and more than ordinary resignation and blessed frame of mind. She died the 14th to our unspeakable sorrow and affliction, and not to our's only, but that of all who knew her, who were many of the best quality, greatest and most virtuous persons . . .

As he did for little Richard, he appends a long catalogue of Mary's qualities and achievements, but we are sensible of the loss anyway, particularly when Mary's sister follows her half a year later:

August 27th, 1685 My daughter Elizabeth died of the small-pox, soon after having married a young man, nephew of Sir John Tippett, Surveyor of the Navy, and one of the Commissioners. The 30th, she was buried in the church at Deptford. Thus, in less than six months were we deprived of two children for our unworthiness and causes best known to God, whom I beseech from the bottom of my heart that He will give us grace to make that right use of all these chastisements, that we may become better, and entirely submit in all things to His infinite wise disposal. Amen!

Fate, however, still had one more grief to bring him, for he had six sons, none of whom survived him and only one of whom (John) reached manhood:

March 24th, 1699 My only remaining son died after a tedious languishing sickness, contracted in Ireland, and increased here, to my exceeding grief and affliction; leaving me one grandson, now at Oxford, whom I pray God to prosper and be the support of the Wotton family. He was aged forty-four years and about three months. He had been six years one of the Commissioners of the Revenue in Ireland, with great ability and reputation.

It is important, however, to see Evelyn's diary as a testament not to death but to life. We can share the sadness of his losses but also enjoy his acute awareness and observation of his fellow creatures, and their deeds and foibles, even at their most gory and cruel.

October 17th, 1660 Scot, Scroop, Cook, and Jones, suffered for reward of their iniquities at Charing Cross, in sight of the place where they put to death their natural prince, and in the presence of the King his son, whom they also sought to kill. I saw not their execution, but met their quarters, mangled, and cut, and reeking, as they were brought from the gallows in baskets on the hurdle. Oh, the miraculous providence of God!

May 30th, 1662 The Queen arrived with a train of Portuguese ladies in their monstrous fardingales, or guard-infantes, their complexions olivader and sufficiently unagreeable. Her Majesty was in the same habit, her foretop long and turned aside very strangely. She was yet of the handsomest countenance of all the rest, and, though low of stature, prettily shaped, languishing and excellent eyes, her teeth wronging her mouth by sticking a little too far out; for the rest, lovely enough.

February 4th, 1685 ... Thus died King Charles II., of a vigorous and robust constitution, and in all appearance promising a long life. He was a prince of many virtues, and many great imperfections; debonaire, easy of access, not bloody nor cruel; his countenance fierce, his voice great, proper of person, every motion became him; a lover of the sea, and skilful in shipping; not affecting other studies, yet he had a laboratory, and know of many empirical medicines, and the easier mechanical mathematics; he loved lanting and building, and brought in a politer way of living, which passed to luxury and intolerable expense. He had a particular talent in telling a story, and facetious passages, of which he had innumerable; this made some buffoons and vicious wretches too presumptuous and familiar, not worthy the favour they abused. He took delight in having a number of little spaniels follow him and lie in his bed-chamber, where he often suffered the bitches to puppy and give suck, which rendered it very offensive, and indeed made the whole court nasty and stinking. He would doubtless have been an excellent prince, had he been less addicted to women, who made him uneasy, and always in want to supply their unmeasurable profusion, to the detriment of many indigent persons who had signally served both him and his father. He frequently and easily changed favourites to his great prejudice . . .

To read Evelyn is to be reminded of Cezanne's famous judgment of Claude Monet – '. . . only an eye, but *what* an eye!' Of his wife, or of their domestic relationship, we are told nothing. Yet beyond the hedge of his beloved garden is a whole public world of which we know more than ever would have been possible if he had not kept his diary. The smaller secrets locked away in his heart he took to the grave with him. For a great diary, his must surely be the most discreet. If it had been published before he died, no one could have been much embarrassed or hurt even within his family. And yet how much poorer our heritage from the past if we had had no Evelyn as eye-witness. Could there possibly be more graphic images than those conjured by his account of the Great Fire of London of 1666?

September 3rd, 1666 . . . The conflagration was so universal, and the people so astonished, that, from the beginning, I know not by what despondency, or fate, they hardly stirred to quench it; so that there was nothing heard, or seen, but crying out and lamentation, running about like distracted creatures, without at all attempting to save even their goods; such a strange consternation there was upon them, so as it burned both in breadth and length, the churches, public halls, Exchange, hospitals, monuments, and ornaments; leaping after a prodigious manner, from house to house, and street to street, at great distances one from the other. For the heat, with a long set of fair and warm weather, had even ignited the air, and prepared the materials to conceive the fire, which devoured, after an incredible manner, houses, furniture, and every thing. Here, we saw the Thames covered with goods floating, all the barges and boats laden with what some had time and courage to save, as, on the other side, the carts, &c., carrying out to the fields, which for many miles were strewed with moveables of all sorts, and tents erecting to shelter both people and what goods they could get away. Oh, the miserable and calamitous spectacle! such as haply the world had not seen since the foundation of it, nor can be outdone till the universal conflagration thereof. All the sky was of a fiery aspect, like the top of a burning oven, and the light seen above forty miles round – about for many nights. God grant mine eyes may never behold the like, who now saw above 10,000 houses all in one flame! The noise and cracking and thunder of the impetuous flames, the shrieking of women and children, the hurry of people, the fall of towers, houses, and churches, was like a hideous storm; and the air all about so hot and inflamed, that at the last one was not able to approach it, so that they were forced to stand still, and let the flames burn on, which they did, for near two miles in length and one in breadth. The clouds also of smoke were dismal, and reached upon computation, near fifty miles in length. Thus, I left it this afternoon burning, a resemblance of Sodom, or the last day ... London was, but is no more! Thus, I returned.

The immediacy of the description, and impression conveyed of the magnitude of the sounds and sights of a holocaust scarcely equalled by Hitler's firebombs in the Second World War blitz on London, leave no doubt in my mind that even if one cannot give John Evelyn the accolade of greatness for literature, he ranks as one of the greatest journalists ever to put pen to paper. Only an eye perhaps, but *what* an eye!

Extraordinary as it may seem now, Evelyn's greatest work had to await the nineteenth century before it saw the light of day. A literary antiquary called William Upcott was employed by Lady Evelyn to inspect the manuscripts at Wotton House, near Dorking in Surrey, papers which had been handed down in the family to John Evelyn's great-great-grandson Sir Frederick Evelyn. Upcott was particularly taken with some diary volumes which he found in a clothes basket. He advised publication and William Bray was called in as editor. Neither Sir Frederick nor Lady Evelyn were alive to see the first publication in 1818 of the diaries, so they were not to know that their distinguished ancestor was to achieve a fame and stature even surpassing the reputation he made for himself during his own lifetime. In 1818 the diaries were a literary sensation and they have scarcely ever been out of print in one form or another since, a triumph denied greater artists than he. For him, the eyes have it.

BIBLIOGRAPHY

John Evelyn: *The Diary of John Evelyn*, edited by William Bray. Revised edition in 2 volumes, Everyman Library (Dent), 1966.

FOUR

The Civil Servant

The rediscovery and publication of Evelyn's diaries provoked much interest from the general reading public. For
a few scholars, however, there was a reawakening of interest
in one of Evelyn's acquaintances, Mr Samuel Pepys. Of
him Evelyn had said, on 26 May 1703:

> This day dies Mr. Samuel Pepys, a very worthy, indus-
> trious and curious person, none in England exceeding
> him in knowledge of the navy, in which he had passed
> through all the most considerable offices, Clerk of the
> Acts and Secretary of the Admiralty, all which he per-
> formed with great integrity ... he was universally
> beloved, hospitable, generous, learned in many things,
> skilled in music, a very great cherisher of learned men of
> whom he had the conversation ... Mr. Pepys had been
> for near forty years so much my particular friend ...

A century had passed since Evelyn and his friends had
mourned the passing of congenial Sam Pepys, and the man
had presumably found his minor niche in history – a modest
reputation even in his own time, a Fellow of the Royal
Society, and a minor civil servant to be given some credit
for moral actions in a venal age. If the name Pepys meant
anything else at all, it was only to Magdalene men, for at
that Cambridge college his collection of books and prints
had been housed at his behest. Among these seventeenth-
century memorabilia was a set of six mysterious manuscript
journals, gathering dust on the shelves, and – this is the
crucial point – totally incomprehensible to the casual browser.
They were written in a quaint and obscure shorthand system

to which the key had been long lost. Whatever secrets they held they were likely to retain.

The interest created by the publication of Evelyn's *magnum opus* did, on the other hand, mean that some attempt should be made. An undergraduate with the distinctly mundane appellation of John Smith was given the task. A consultation with the celebrated contemporary stenographer W. B. Gurney brought the memorable verdict that the task would be impossible. Perhaps if the undergraduate had been one whit less determined than Smith, Gurney would have been correct. Smith worked for the next three years at the rate of twelve to fourteen hours a day, cracked the cipher and produced a worthy and comprehensive transcript. To him should go the credit for transforming an obscure naval clerk into one of the most famous Englishmen of all time, the civil servant into one of literature's brightest gems.

Smith did not receive full credit for his herculean efforts on Pepys's behalf. When the first edition of Pepys's diary was published together with some Pepysian letters, a more aristocratic name was needed on the title page, so the volume which appeared in 1825 had Lord Braybrooke as editor designate. In fact, Lord Braybrooke's editorial industry had been confined to ruthlessly excising any entry that failed to accord with his own opinions or prejudices. The book still raced through three printings, as the reading public realized that despite the distorting offices of Lord Braybrooke, a new and uniquely authentic voice was making itself heard. An expanded version was published in 1848–9 incorporating about a quarter more of the original, a re-editing was carried out in 1854, and new extracts included in a Bohn library edition of 1858. In 1875–9 the Reverend Mynors Bright made a new transcript from the manuscripts, and it was this transcription that was the basis of H. B. Wheatley's large edition of 1893–9. This edition, with numerous inaccuracies, consisted of most of Bright's transcript, except for a number of 'unprintable' passages.

This is but to mention the major editions. In addition there were a hundred and more selections from the diaries printed and reprinted and circulating over the whole world.

The reception of the original publication in 1825 was generally enthusiastic. Sir Walter Scott's voice was raised in its favour in the *Quarterly Review* and he himself was to take to the diary form before the end of his prolific life. The editor of the *Edinburgh Review*, Francis Jeffrey, was against, but then he is now remembered, if at all, as the upholder of writers with old-fashioned and neo-classic values, and for damning with faint praise the work of Wordsworth and Coleridge. Jeffrey's strictures were set aside as if never uttered; Pepys, from 1825 on and ever since, was a best-seller.

It is the distinction of any masterpiece, be it a painting, a poem, a book, a play or whatever, to survive the trivial and fleeting successes of fashion. Time is our greatest ally in separating the wheat from the chaff, and within a master-piece, successive generations will find something that speaks uniquely to them. To give a spectacular example, the meaning and treatment of Shakespeare's *King Lear* can be seen to vary incredibly according to the viewpoint of the time – for instance, that of an Elizabethan would differ radically from that of a contemporary of Garrick's in the eighteenth century, and that of a contemporary of Irving's in the nineteenth century would bear little resemblance to that of Jan Kott in our own time. The one constant, give or take a few textual editings, in this succession of images now classical, now romantic, now antiquarian, now meta-physical, is the play *King Lear* itself. The play has not changed, only attitudes to it.

This digression on matters theatrical, on which that inveterate play-goer Samuel Pepys would have had his own strong opinions were he still with us, is by way of an introduction to the fact that our present age is the very first able to read Pepys's diary as it was originally written. We would resent, quite rightly, any attempt to choose for us what parts we shall or shall not read. Leaving aside all other considerations (for censorship is a complex and confusing issue), this is what the abandonment of thou-shalt-nots is all about. Even those who would advocate wholesale extensions of moral censorship of what we shall hear, see or read, invariably make it clear that what worries them is not what they themselves might hear, see or read, but what *others* more corruptible than they might make of it all. What is sauce for Mr Griffith Jones is not to be sauce for wives and servants.

Concern for the moral welfare of the reading public has meant, indirectly, that it is only in the 1970s that it begins to be possible to publish the whole of Pepys. Starting in 1970–1, a magnificent publishing project by G. Bell and Sons, the London publishers, has been to issue the entire contents of a new transcription of the famous diaries. The eventual complete edition will comprise nine volumes of text and explanatory footnotes, together with a volume of commentary and a volume of index. It is a magnificent example of Anglo-American scholarship, jointly edited by Robert Latham, a Fellow of Magdalene College (how pleased Pepys would have been about that!), and William Matthews, a Professor of English at the University of California. Robert Latham's scholarly devotion to Pepys has been every bit equal to that of poor John Smith's, and William Matthews would have already earned undying gratitude for his bibliographies of diaries alone.

They have painstakingly restored the Pepysian spellings and pungent phrases of three thousand manuscript pages, making their text the most faithful ever published and one which is unlikely to be superseded. The quality of accuracy and scholarship has to be stressed lest I erroneously give the impression that the restoration of nearly a hundred short paragraphs dealing mainly with Pepys's sexual goings-on is the main purpose of the exercise. The function of the erudition is not to treat us to 'the dirty bits', but to enable us to read exactly what Pepys wrote.

The successive volumes are expensive so there is unlikely to be a runaway sale for them to prurient searchers
for erotica. It is likely that a paperback selection mainly
devoted to titillating extracts of Pepysian peccadilloes
might appear in due course, but one cannot see the phenomenal sales of the book during the nineteenth century being
paralleled. After Lady Chatterley and her literary descen-
dants, it would need more than Pepys's sexuality, inter-
spersed with a modicum of decorous wife-bashing, to reap
a *succès de scandale*. What was it then, that the Victorians,
early, mid and late, found so attractive about nine years in
the life of our hero? (The diary was kept only from 1
January 1660 to 31 May 1669, the entry for the latter date
testifying that the diarist gave up because of his fast failing
eyesight:

> And this ends all that I doubt I shall ever be able to do
> with my own eyes in the keeping of my journal, I being
> not able to do it any longer, having done now so long
> as to undo my eyes almost every time that I take a pen
> in my hand; and, therefore, whatever comes of it, I
> must forbear ... which is almost as much as to see
> myself go into my grave: for which, and all the dis-
> comforts that will accompany my being blind, the good
> God prepare me!)

Leaving aside for the moment the obvious interest of
Victorian historians and those with a specialist interest in
some aspect of the particular world in which Pepys lived
and worked, surely one of the main reasons that his diary
held its great popular appeal throughout the century was
that his career was such a fine example of material success
through self-help. Here was a perfect model of an English
gentleman from the past showing all the cardinal virtues
of self-reliance and careful accountancy, yet confiding all his
minor trangressions to his diary for all the world to read
a century and more later. The tired nineteenth-century

businessman could lay down his account books, pick up his volume of Pepys and read admiringly of the doings of a conscientious official reaping the rewards of his industry. This was all rather inspiring. On the other hand, Pepys was a deal more acceptable than most of the pedestalled paragons, because he, unlike most Victorians and indeed unlike most of us today, was not concerned to show himself in a good light or to put a priggish front on his misdemeanours: the Victorian businessman could look and admire, but feel just that little bit superior too.

Where Pepys showed himself to be petulant or irritable, the Victorian saw himself as one who dispensed righteous wrath. Where Pepys showed himself to be vain over his appearance, the Victorian saw himself as an upholder of the correct sartorial standards becoming his social position. And where Pepys gave his wife a back-hander, the Victorian could draw a certain vicarious pleasure, but would know subconsciously that his own wife was in such a subservient social and legal position that so crude a measure need never become necessary.

The transformation of Pepys from the penniless clerk with barely two sovereigns to rub together to the naval official of some substance very conveniently coincides with the keeping of the diary. The following entries should make the speed of the ascent clear:

May 30th, 1660 . . . All this morning making up my accounts, in which I counted that I had made myself now worth about £80, at which my heart was glad and blessed God . . .

June 3rd, 1660 . . . At sermon in the morning: after dinner into my cabin to cast my accounts up, and find myself to be worth near £100, for which I bless Almighty God, it being more than I hoped for so soon, being, I believe, not clearly worth £25 when I came to sea, besides my house and goods.

July 7th, 1660 . . . I took an order for the advance of the

salaries of the officers of the Navy, and mine is raised to
£350 per annum.

May 30th, 1662 This morning I made up my accounts,
and find myself *de claro* worth about £530, and no more,
so little have I increased it since my last reckoning [i.e.
£500 in May 1661], but I confess I have laid out much
money in clothes . . .

May 31st, 1663 . . . I to make up my month's accounts,
and find myself clear worth £726 . . .

May 31st, 1664 . . . I find myself come to £930.

June 4th, 1665 Blessed be God! am worth £1400 odd
money . . .

May 30th, 1666 I after dinner to even all my accounts of
this month, and bless God! I find myself, notwithstanding great expenses of late; (viz. £80 now to pay for a
necklace; near £40 for a set of chairs and couch, near
£40 for my three pictures) yet do I gather, and am now
worth £5,200 . . .

May 30, 1667 . . . I am now worth £6,700 . . .

It takes nothing away from Pepys's undoubted worth as
a good official to point out that the Restoration of Charles
II in 1660 brought many similar success stories in its wake.
In 1659, the year before the diary opens, Pepys had gone
to the Baltic to join the squadron of Edward Mountagu.
Mountagu was Pepys's cousin who was made General of
the Fleet, and although he had started his career as one of
Cromwell's colonels, he was a royalist at heart and well
placed to reap the benefits of England's return to a
monarchy. In March 1660 Pepys became his cousin's
private secretary. Mountagu was destined to become the
Earl of Sandwich and as 'my Lord' (as he is described in
the diary) went up the social and financial ladder, he made
sure enough perks and offices fell into his cousin's lap to
share the family's new good fortune.

Thus it was that after a new Parliament had in April
1660 invited Charles II to return from exile, in May a

fleet left for The Hague to fetch the new king and Pepys
went with them. He first met with Charles there on 17 May:

> we kissed his, and the Duke of York's, and the Princess
> Royal's hands. The King seems to be a very sober man;
> and a very splendid Court he hath in the number of
> persons of quality that are about him, English, very rich
> in habit . . .

The King returned in triumph and it was not long before
his friends were duly rewarded. In July Pepys obtained a
Patent as Clerk of the Acts to the Navy, a post all the more
gratifying because it brought a new house along with it.

> *July 15th, 1660* . . . My wife and I mightily pleased with
> our new house that we hope to have. My patent has cost
> me a great deal of money, about £40, which is the only
> thing at present which do trouble me much.

In his new house at Seething Lane, he soon found £40 a
worthwhile investment (in Pepys's day, anything that could
be bought and sold, including jobs, was), and he was to
add a number of other offices to it: Commissioner for
Tangier in 1661, Treasurer of the Tangier Committee in
1665, Surveyor-General of Victualling in 1666. (In the
years after his diary came to an end, he was to become
Secretary for Admiralty Affairs and Member of Parliament.)
Pepys did not expect his journal to be read in his own
lifetime unless, as Robert Louis Stevenson once suggested,
it was by himself in old age. Part of its uncanny appeal is
that it is a secretive and idiosyncratic monologue, written
hastily to capture his inner thoughts before they were
beyond recall. It is perhaps the best self-portrait in literature, telling all without the desire to impress that one
senses in, say, Rousseau's *Confessions*. For whom was it
written then? It is impossible to know. For whom did
Rembrandt paint his self-portraits?
It is not Rembrandt, however, who comes to mind in
considering Pepys, but rather the school of interior painters

among Rembrandt's countrymen, the de Hoochs and the Vermeers. Like them, Pepys has the ability to give us a succession of everyday images, faithfully yet exquisitely drawn, capturing for eternity the transient quality of the moment, and building each upon each to a satisfying whole. To absorb the full splendour of a Vermeer, one has to see the entire canvas, and a selection of small details does scant justice to the overall design. There is no overall design in Pepys in the same sense (a diarist, after all, paints day by day without knowledge of what the next day may bring), yet his details build up to an entity – Pepys the man, warts and all – in just the same way. Therefore, neither selected extracts nor bowdlerized entries can quite convey the full rounded flavour of the man or his diary.

Take, for example, Pepys's relationship with his wife. Was it a good marriage or a bad one? What he writes of her in the diary is often contradictory and complex, veering from pride and love to vexation and incomprehension; and her attitudes to him are equally mercurial if his words are to be believed. That this confusion should exist is surely a tribute to the value of the diary, and the quality of the truth contained within it. 'My wife and I have never had a cross word in ten years', writes the autobiographer, blithely forgetting the scrap on 18 February 1964, and the flash of irritability on Boxing Day, 1967. The diarist cannot be so selective: there it is in black and white, the scrap in 1964 and the sharp word in 1967 captured for all time unless the entries are ignored or destroyed. Instead of a selective view of Pepys's marriage seen through the distorting lens of hindsight, we have access to his outlook on a daily basis, unmodified by reflection.

For an ambitious man, it had not been the most advantageous of marriages. The future Elizabeth Pepys was the impecunious and impractical fifteen-year-old daughter of an equally penniless Huguenot when Pepys had fallen for her. He was twenty-two. By the time the diary opens, they had been married for five years, time enough for the first

3

romantic flush to have worn off, and for irritations at each other's foibles to have increased to the point of friction, Friction was sometimes uppermost:

December 19, 1661 . . . My wife and I went home by coach; but in the way I took occasion to fall out with my wife very highly about her ribbons being ill matched and of two colours; and to very high words, so that, like a passionate fool, I did call her a bad name, for which I was afterwards sorry.

And in May of 1663, he got very worried about the attentions paid her by her dancing master, Pemberton:

May 16th, 1663 After dinner comes Pemberton, and I being out of humour would not see him, pretending business, but Lord; with what jealousy did I walk up and down my chamber listening to whether they danced or no. So to my office awhile, and, my jealousy still reigning . . .

Abuse could extend beyond the verbal too:

April 5th, 1664 . . . she answering me some way that I did not like, I pulled her by the nose; indeed, to offend her, though afterward, to appease her, I denied it, but only it was done in jest. The poor wretch took it mighty ill; and I believe, besides wringing her nose, she did feel pain and so cried a great while . . .

December 7th, 1666 . . . and I by coach home to dinner; where finding the cloth laid and much crumpled but clean, I grew angry and flung the trenchers about the room, and in a mighty heat I was . . .

December 19, 1664 . . . And from our people's being forced to take the key to go out to light a candle, I was very angry and began to find fault with my wife for not commanding her servants as she ought. Thereupon, she giving me some cross answer, I did strike her over her left eye such a blow, as the poor wretch did cry out and was in great pain; but her spirit was such as to endeavour to bite and scratch me . . .

This last gives us some indication that Mrs Pepys did not always take kindly to *his* behaviour, but rather gave as good as she got. (Often it is clear, even through his eyes alone, that some of her behaviour – slack accounting, gossiping, untidiness – was conceived deliberately to provoke him. She, one senses, was always the real victor in this battle of the sexes.)

March 28th, 1665 Taking my wife's kitchen accounts, and there found 7s. wanting, which did occasion a very high falling out between us, I indeed, too angrily insisting upon so poor a thing, and did give her very provoking words, calling her 'beggar' and reproaching her friends, which she took very stomachfully and reproached me justly with mine. I find she is very cunning, and, when she least shows it, has her wit at work . . .

January 12th, 1669 . . . This evening I observed my wife mighty dull, and I myself was not mighty fond, because of some hard words she did give me at noon out of a jealousy at my being abroad this morning . . . but I to bed, not thinking but she would come after me. But waking by and by out of a slumber, which I usually fall into presently after my coming into bed, I found she did not prepare to come to bed, but got fresh candles, and more wood for her fire, it being mighty cold, too. At this being troubled, I after a while prayed her to come to bed; so, after an hour or two, she silent, and I now and then praying her to come to bed, she fell out into a fury, that I was a rogue and false to her. I did, as I might truly, deny it, and was mightily troubled, but all would not serve. At last, about one o'clock, she came to my side of the bed and drew my curtain open, and with the tongs red hot at the end made as if she did design to pinch me with them: at which, in dismay, I rose up, and with a few words she laid them down, and did little

by little, very sillily, let all the discourse fall; and about
two, but with much seeming difficulty, came to bed, and
there lay well all night, and long in bed talking together
with much pleasure, it being, I know, nothing but her
doubt of my going out yesterday without telling her of
my going, which did vex her, poor wretch! last night;
and I cannot blame her jealousy, though it do vex me to
the heart.

Game, set and match to Mrs Pepys?
    Such militancy on either side was fortunately rare and I
think we would be justified in drawing the conclusion
from most of the diary that their marriage was very firmly
based on a wealth of love for one another, and although
there were jealousies on either side (in her case, often
justified by his latest dalliance among the ranks of actresses
or servants) they rankled because both partners fundamentally cared. Pepys always knew that she had married
him not as a socialite of some standing, but as a penniless
nonentity. He makes the point himself:

February 25th, 1667 Lay long in bed, talking with pleasure
with my poor wife, how she used to make coal fires, and
wash my foul clothes with her own hand for me, poor
wretch! in our little room at my Lord Sandwich's; for
which I ought for ever to love and admire her, and do;
and persuade myself she would do the same thing again,
if God should reduce us to it . . .

In our own post-Freudian times, there is something
infinitely refreshing about Pepys's Chaucerian frankness.
He treats his continuing sexual appetite, his momentary
bodily disorder, his defecatory and urinary functions, his
wife's menstrual discomforts, and his erotic dreams of
Lady Castlemaine, all with such openness and in such
matter-of-fact terms that even if the details would win
him no friends in polite drawing-rooms, he is never
offensive in the slightest. There is no smut, no snigger

behind the hand, no desire to do anything but to set down the truth without self-deception, and this, remember, in an age of almost unparalleled licence in the court and its social adjunct, the theatre. If there is one quality to appeal to us now, as his financial and social successes appealed to Victorians, one hopes this would be it. It is the quality we can least afford to ignore.

As with the diary of his friend John Evelyn, there are in addition incidental pleasures. Firstly, where Evelyn tended to regard the liberal mores of the court of Charles II with fastidious or priggish disdain, Pepys, in the theatre at least, relished the new plays, the new actresses (Pepys's age was first in which female roles were taken by actresses), and the personalities on the stage or in the audience – even if they misbehaved:

January 28th, 1661 ... and thence to the Theatre, where I saw again 'the Lost Lady' which doth now please me better than before. And here, I sitting behind in a dark place, a lady spat backward upon me by a mistake, not seeing me. But after seeing her to be a very pretty lady, I was not troubled at it at all.

Pepys, who devoted much of his new wealth to supporting his visits to the theatre, is one of our most important sources for our knowledge of Restoration theatre. We know from other historical sources that 'theatre' at that time meant either the King's Company of players who played at the new Drury Lane theatre from 1663 onwards, or another company under Sir William Davenant, but it is only Pepys who gives us such distinct and individual cameos of plays and players:

September 29th, 1662 ... and then to the King's Theatre, where we saw 'Midsummer's Night's Dream', which I had never seen before, nor shall ever again, for it is the most insipid, ridiculous play that ever I saw in my life ...

March 1st, 1662 . . . saw 'Romeo and Juliet', the first time it was ever acted [i.e. in this production], but it is a play of itself the worst that ever I heard, and the worst acted that ever I saw these people do, and I am resolved to go no more to see the first time of acting, for they were all of them out more or less . . .

If there were these occasional disappointments, there were also compensations – music, for example;

February 27th, 1668 With my wife to the King's House, to see 'The Virgin Martyr', the first time it hath been acted a great while, and it is mighty pleasant: not that the play is worth much, but it is finely acted by Beck Marshall. But that which did please me beyond anything in the whole world was the wind-music when the angel comes down, which is so sweet that it ravished me, and indeed, in a word, did wrap up my soul so that it made me really sick (just as I have formerly been when in love with my wife), that neither then, nor all the evening going home, and at home, I was able to think of anything, but remained all night transported, so as I could not believe that ever any music that hath that real command over the soul of a man as this did upon me . . .

And the best compensation of all was a glimpse of Nell Gwynn, or Beck Marshall, or his good friend Mrs Knipp, all actresses:

April 3rd, 1665 . . . All the pleasure of the play was, the King and my Lady Castlemaine were there; and pretty witty Nell, at the King's House, and the younger Marshall sat next us; which pleased me mightily.

February 2nd, 1669 . . . that that pleased me most in the play [i.e. *The Heiress*] is the first song that Knipp sings, she singing three or four; and, indeed, it was very finely sung, so as to make the whole house clap her . . . My wife in mighty ill humour all night, and in the morning

I found it to be from her observing Knipp to wink and smile on me, and she says I smiled on her; and, poor wretch! I did perceive that she did, and do on all such occasions, mind my eyes. I did with much difficulty pacify her, and we were friends, she desiring that hereafter, at that house, we might always sit either above in a box, or, if there be no room, close up to the lower boxes.

There is scarcely any aspect of life about which we cannot glean something from the pages of Pepys. Reading the whole work, one is totally absorbed into his world, so strange yet so familiar. The final brief extract, taken from a long account of the Great Fire of 1666, has been chosen because it contrasts so well with Evelyn's account in Chapter Three, illuminating the differing concerns of the two friends. Whereas Evelyn had the reporter's concern to present the whole dramatic sweep of the canvas Pepys, the artist and humanist, never allows personal intimacy to lose out to the public event (although Pepys was the man who reported the course of the fire to the king and his brother):

September 2nd, 1666 ... So I went down to the waterside, and there got a boat, and through bridge, and there saw a lamentable fire. Poor Michell's house, as far as the Old Swan, already burned that way, and the fire running further, that, in a very little time, it got as far as the Steelyard, while I was there. Everybody endeavouring to remove their goods, and flinging into the river or bringing them into lighters that lay off; poor people staying in their houses as long as till the very fire touched them, and then running into boats, or clambering from one pair of stairs by the waterside to another. And, among other things, the poor pigeons, I perceive, were loth to leath their houses, but hovered about the windows and balconies, till they, some of them, burned their wings, and fell down ...

Evelyn the journalist also saw the flames and the people taking to the water to avoid them, but only Pepys, with a novelist's awareness of telling details, noticed the pigeons.

BIBLIOGRAPHY

Samuel Pepys: *The Diary of Samuel Pepys*, edited from Mynors Bright by John Warrington. Revised and reset in 3 volumes (Everyman Library, Dent, 1958); *The Diary of Samuel Pepys*, a new and complete transcription by Robert Latham and William Matthews. In progress 1970 by Bell.

FIVE

The Man from Scotland

If the diaries of Pepys could have been hidden away from the world for over 120 years after his death, then anything can happen in the way of literary discoveries. If there has been anything of a parallel in our own times it must be the emergence of James Boswell as a diarist of extraordinary merit, and moreover prolific enough to put even the energies of Pepys to shame. That this should be so stems from a chain of events no less remarkable than the deciphering of the Pepys shorthand.

When Boswell died in 1795, he was known to have left a large number of private papers; for a man so inexhaustably interested in himself, this was hardly surprising. When we look a little more closely at his life, we will see to what extent he was at odds with his family. Born in 1740, the eldest son of the 8th Laird of Auchinleck, neither his ambitions nor his behaviour gained him much of a family reputation. However, when his executors met (three distinguished gentlemen – Sir William Forbes, Edmond Malone, and the Reverend William J. Temple), they had to guard against offending the Boswell family while bearing in mind posterity's claim to know every detail about its literary heroes. Perhaps unable to balance satisfactorily the claim of one against the other, they reached a compromise solution: to postpone any publication until Boswell's own son was old enough to decide for himself. The papers were deposited at the family home, but rumours of their frankness circulated, and it became generally believed that they had been destroyed.

There the matter rested until the late 1820s. A literary

specialist in the eighteenth century, John Wilson Croker, who was compiling a new edition of Boswell's *Life of Johnson*, made tentative enquiries as to whether material was still extant for his edition, but no material became available. When Croker's book was eventually published in 1831, Macaulay reviewed it, at length, for *The Edinburgh Review*. The critique achieved great fame, though it was not entirely fair, being as effective a demolition job as could be wished: Macaulay compared Croker's work with Dr Johnson's leg of mutton ('as bad as bad could be, ill fed, ill killed, ill kept, and ill dressed'), saying it was 'ill compiled, ill arranged, ill written, and ill printed'.

This was not all. Once started, there was not much that could stop Macaulay's steam-roller, and having flattened the editor, it promptly proceeded to flatten the biographer. Having conceded that the *Life* was the greatest of biographies, Lord M. argued that it had been written by 'one of the smallest men that ever lived . . .' He thundered:

a man of the meanest and feeblest intellect . . . He was the laughing-stock of that brilliant society which has owed to him the greater part of its fame. He was always laying himself at the feet of some eminent man, and begging to be spit upon and trampled upon . . . Servile and impertinent, shallow and pedantic, a bigot and a sot, bloated with family pride, and eternally blustering about the dignity of a born gentleman, yet stooping to be a tale-bearer, an eavesdropper, a common butt in the taverns of London . . . Everything which another man would have hidden, everything the publication of which would have another man hang himself, was a matter of gay and clamorous exultation to his weak and diseased mind . . . All the caprices of his temper, all the illusions of his vanity, all his hypochondriac whimsies, all his castles in the air, he displayed with a cool self-complacency, a perfect unconsciousness that he was making a fool of himself, to which it is impossible to find a parallel in the whole history of mankind. He has used many people ill; but assuredly he has used nobody so ill as himself ... he was a dunce, a parasite, and a coxcomb.

It must surely be admitted that the Boswell family, after that review, could hardly be expected to provide more ammunition for Macaulay or any other reviewer to have a second shy at their distinguished ancestor. The Boswell papers, if not destroyed, stayed hidden.

By the dawn of the twentieth century, Boswell's family was represented by two great-granddaughters. One died childless in 1905, the other married an Irish peer, the entire contents of the family home of Auchinleck being transferred across the Irish Sea in 1917 to a castle near Dublin. From that castle, papers began to emerge, though an American professor who tried to gain access to and publish the collection was refused in the mid-1920s. An American collector, however, bought most of the extant papers in 1926 and brought out a private edition, but more manuscripts turned up in a box of croquet equipment(!) in 1930, and more emerged in Scotland in 1937 and 1939. It was not until 1949 that Yale University used Mellon money to buy the entire collection.

From Yale, then, over the last twenty years, a superb edition of Boswell papers, no smaller in scope, and no less scholarly in execution than the Bell Pepys, has been issued. In this country, the edition has been published by William Heinemann, to whom our gratitude should go for enabling us to see the man Boswell in his true colours.

How do his true colours compare with Macaulay's acid palette? It must be admitted that the emergence of Boswell the diarist in one sense confirms most of the things that Macaulay said. However, there is something even more important that Macaulay did not say, which is that although Boswell, perhaps in common with Wagner or Beethoven, may not have been a particularly pleasing companion to meet socially, this does not make his work any less admirable. No one pretends that their work was some kind of freak happening, an intellectual achievement stumbled upon accidentally by a happy idiot. Theoretically, a roomful of monkeys playing snap with Scrabble tiles to infinity could eventually produce all the plays of Shakespeare: the actual likelihood, on the other hand, is small. Similarly, so monumental a masterpiece as Boswell's *Life of Johnson*, at least arguably the finest biography in the English language, cannot be explained away as the scribblings of an alcoholic Scotsman with tape-recorders for eardrums quoting the sayings and doings of his companion.

The publication of Boswell's other journals has confirmed all the promise of the keeper of the *Journal of a Tour to the Hebrides with Samuel Johnson*. This was originally published by Boswell in 1785, the year after Johnson's death, with the express intention of proving his fitness to write the biography of the late lamented Doctor. The journals that have emerged since establish beyond question that what the nineteenth century sought to explain as straight transcriptions of a shorthand note-taker is in fact creative genius of high art, consciously and knowingly reconstructing the inner truth of events, rather than their literal reproduction.

Boswell's genius was for keeping a diary. It appears that many passages of the biography are taken from the journals, sometimes physically removed for the purpose, and that all his important books were reconstructed from his journals. His purpose in keeping a diary, according to his definitive biographer, Frederick A. Pottle, and an interpretation one can readily believe, is that for all Boswell's tremendous zest for living, he was enormously fascinated by the operations of his own mind, to the extent that his experiences were not fully realized until he had defined them and recorded them in his journal. He as good as says so himself: 'I should live no more than I can record, as one should not have more corn growing than one can get in . . .' It is precisely this quality that makes him a great diarist – the ability to regard himself with the same subtle powers of observation that he used for others, and the literary power to recreate his own experiences in vigorous prose. If we can pay tribute to Pepys for his ability to give us a self-portrait, un-retouched, then we cannot withhold admiration for Boswell when he does the same thing. If the subject is less sympathetic, that is more than out-weighed by Boswell's extraordinary ability to hold our attention. Where Pepys gives us a wealth of social detail and an honesty nicely bounded by tact, Boswell gives us himself in the raw, a sort of objective history of the inner man, an inner man that a lesser writer and observer would be compelled to pretend did not exist.

Boswell's troubles began early in life. Being the eldest son of a strong and intolerant father unwilling to see his son develop other than in the way *he* wanted, made him a timid child subject to depression which culminated in something akin to a nervous breakdown at the age of seventeen. After this crisis, he ironically blossomed into a gregarious rake. There is surely something compulsive about the way he chose to assert himself in all the ways his father would most strongly disapprove. He chased actresses indiscriminately, and whereas his father wanted him to devote himself to the law, he wanted to become an officer in the Guards. This latter desire was no normal military ambition. Boswell did not see himself in terms of glorious deeds on the battlefield. It was rather a case of such a profession necessitating his presence in London, and therefore beyond parental control, and the metropolis being full of actresses and ladies of quality perhaps ready to welcome him to their beds.

He made one trip to London in 1760, and before his father could engineer his return to Scotland, he had savoured *la dolce vita* and liked what he found. There followed three years of strife at home with Boswell trying to get back to London, and his father trying to press him to a legal career. As a compromise solution, he was allowed to return to London for a time, providing he passed a law examination in the spring of 1762. He passed it and left for London with an allowance of £100.

Perhaps because he knew few people in London initially, he found the time to make his London journal of 1762–3 very full indeed. The entries were written up and sent to a friend in Scotland for safe keeping, and it may well be that they are more polished and dramatic as a result of this one-man audience. It is possible too that he was determined not to let it be thought that his presence in London, for which he had striven so hard, could in any way fail to come up to expectations. One particular series of entries, quoted below, would make a brilliant true short story in their own right.

After almost succumbing to a street-woman in the Strand in November, but deciding the dangers of venereal infection were too great, he resolved to wait until he 'got some safe girl or was liked by some women of fashion'. By 14 December he has met 'Louisa', a Covent Garden actress.

> This lady has been indisposed and saw no company, but today I was admitted. She was in a pleasing undress and looked very pretty. She received me with great politeness . . .

Two days later, he pays another visit, 'informing her by my looks of my passion for her . . .'. Next day, he discreetly finds out that she has no beau and they exchange pleasantries:

> 'I hope we shall be better acquainted and like one another better.' 'Come, Sir, let us talk no more of that now.' 'No, Madam, I will not. It is like giving the book in the preface.'

and the banter continues until he takes his leave: ' "Sir, you are welcome here as often as you please." "Madam, I am infinitely obliged to you." ' Next day he returns: 'I then went to Louisa's. I was really in love. I felt a warmth at my heart which glowed at my face . . .'

On the 19th, he is chatty and gay 'with looking at so fine a woman and thinking what delight I should have with her . . .'. On the 20th, she borrows two guineas from him:

> On Saturday I just kissed her hand. She now sung to me. I got up in raptures and kissed her with great warmth. She received this very genteelly. I had a delicacy in presuming too far, lest it should look like demanding goods for my money . . .

Such considerations did not prevent him from continuing his suit on the 22nd, with the following response: ' "Nay, dear Sir" (I pressing her to me and kissing her now and then) "pray be quiet. Such a thing requires time to consider of . . .".' She stalls again on the 24th ('I was quite confused') but is more promising on the 26th:

> She said that we should take time to consider of it, and that then we could determine how to act. We agreed that the time should be a week, and that if I remained of the same opinion, she would then make me blessed . . .

By 1 January 1763 the week is up, and he is pressing his suit:

> 'Ah, Madam!' 'Nay, but you are an encroaching creature!' (Upon this I advanced to the greatest freedom by a sweet elevation of the charming petticoat.) 'Good Heaven, Sir!' 'Madam, I cannot help it. I adore you. Do you like me?' (She answered me with a warm kiss and pressing me to her bosom, sighed 'O Mr. Boswell.') . . .

The opportunity is not quite right for the affair to be followed to its logical conclusion, but Boswell is asked to return next day when Louisa's landlady is at church.

Unfortunately, when the happy hour arrives, Boswell's spirit is willing but the flesh surprisingly weak:

> I sat down, I toyed with her. Yet I was not inspired by Venus. I felt rather a delicate sensation of love than a violent amorous inclination for her. I was very miserable. I thought myself feeble as a gallant, although I had experienced the reverse many a time, Louisa knew not my powers. She might imagine me impotent. I sweated almost with anxiety, which made me worse . . . The time of church was almost elapsed when I began to feel that I was still a man. I fanned the flame by pressing her alabaster breasts and kissing her delicious lips. I then barred the door of her dining-room, led her all fluttering into her bedchamber, and was just making a triumphal entry when we heard her landlady coming up. 'O Fortune why did it happen thus?' would have been the exclamation of a Roman bard. We were stopped most suddenly and cruelly from the fruition of each other. She ran out and stopped the landlady from coming up . . .

Rather than risk a recurrence of so frustrating a sequence of events, next day Boswell pressed her to join him on neutral ground: '. . . I insisted that she should go and pass the night with me somewhere. She begged time to think of it . . .'.

On the Tuesday, he finds a rendezvous and she promises to join him there on the following Saturday or Sunday. She then cries off, with reason: '. . . I understood that Nature's periodical effects on the human, or more properly female, constitution forbade it . . .'.

On 9 January, Boswell records that they have decided on the following Wednesday: 'Wednesday without fail . . . the happy night.' Wednesday arrives at last:

> I came softly into the room, and in a sweet delirium slipped into bed and was immediately clasped into her

snowy arms and pressed to her milk-white bosom. Good heavens, what a loose we did give to our amorous dalliance! The friendly curtain of darkness concealed our blushes. In a moment I felt myself animated with the strongest powers of love, and, from my dearest creature's kindness, had a most luscious feast. Proud of my god-like vigour, I soon resumed the noble game. I was in full glow of health ... A more voluptuous night I never enjoyed. Five times was I fairly lost in supreme rapture. Louisa was madly fond of me; she declared I was a prodigy, and asked me if this was not extraordinary for human nature. I said twice as much might be, but this was not, although in my own mind I was somewhat proud of my performance ...

It must be admitted that he does the scene full justice, though he adds: '... I have painted this night as well as I could. The description is faint; but I surely may be styled a Man of Pleasure.' Next day too, he remains well pleased with himself:

I really conducted this affair with a manliness and a prudence that pleased me very much. The whole expense was just eighteen shillings ...

The affair continues, if not at the same fever pitch. On the 16th: 'I went to Louisa and was permitted the rites of love with great complacency; yet I felt my passion for Louisa much gone ...' Similarly, the next day: 'I ... again had full fruition of her charms. I still, though, found that the warm enthusiasm of love was over ...' Despite momentary forebodings, things are better the following day:

January 18th, 1763 I this day began to feel an unaccountable alarm of unexpected evil: a little heat in the members of my body sacred to Cupid, very like the symptoms of that distemper with which Venus, when cross, takes it into her head to plague her votaries. But then I had run no risks. I had been with no woman but Louisa

... Away then with such idle fears, such groundless, uneasy apprehensions! When I came to Louisa's, I felt myself stout and well and most courageously did I plunge into the fount of love, and had vast pleasure ...

Alas, poor Boswell, another day passed and his worst fears are confirmed:

I this morning felt stronger symptoms of the sad distemper, yet I was unwilling to imagine such a thing ... When I got home, though, then came sorrow. Too, too plain was Signor Gonorrhoea ...

There is a flaming row when he taxes Louisa with her treachery, and she denies responsibility with every appearance of sincerity. It is a sadder if not wiser Boswell who records the end of the affair:

... And yet her positive asseverations really stunned me. She is in all probability a most consummate dissembling whore. Thus ended my intrigue with the fair Louisa, which I flattered myself so much with, and from which I expected at least a winter's safe copulation ...

Despite his fear of venereal infection, he was to be *hors de combat* from the visits of his 'Signor Gonorrhoea' on other occasions in the future. (In the spring of 1768, for example, he was confined to his sick-bed for six weeks.) The fear of retribution could never quite overcome the urgent nature of his sexuality, and it seems to me at least that his sexual appetite – the journals abound with conquests ranging from whores in dark alleys to ladies of fashion – was the most spectacular symptom of his feelings of inadequacy. This is the fascinating dichotomy of Boswell's character: Boswell, the man with a dominant father, needing to boost his ego by conquest on the one hand, yet Boswell the diarist, watching and recording as objectively as if he were observing someone else's actions.

Also in his London journal of 1762–3 is an entry relating to what was to become the most important day of his life.

Monday, May 16th, 1763 ... I drank tea at Davies's in Russell Street, and about seven came in the great Mr. Samuel Johnson, whom I have so long wished to see. Mr. Davies introduced me to him. As I knew his mortal antipathy at the Scotch, I cried to Davies, 'Don't tell where I come from'. However, he said, 'From Scotland'. 'Mr. Johnson,' I said, 'indeed I come from Scotland, but I cannot help it.' 'Sir,' replied he, 'that, I find, is what a very great many of your countrymen cannot help'.

It was certainly not the appearance of the good Doctor that impressed the young Boswell:

Mr. Johnson is a man of a most dreadful appearance. He is a very big man, is troubled with sore eyes, the palsy, and the king's evil. He is very slovenly in his dress and speaks with a most uncouth voice. Yet his great knowledge and strength of expression command vast respect and render him very excellent company. He has great humour and is a worthy man. But this dogmatical roughness of manners is disagreeable. I shall mark what I remember of his conversation ...

(By 'palsy' Boswell means a nervous twitch or tic, and by 'king's evil' he means scrofula.)

History now knows to what extent Boswell followed his resolution to record the sayings of Johnson, but it should be emphasized here that in this entry for 16 May, Boswell betrays another factor which contributed to his sense of inadequacy – his nationality. Less than twenty years before, Charles Edward, the Bonnie Prince, and his highland warriors had been marching across the border into England as far as Derby: an event which confirmed beyond question dark English suspicions that the Scots were barbarians not to be trusted in civilized society. Indeed, Boswell's literary style already demonstrates what strenuous efforts he must have made to eliminate Scots dialect from his speech and his prose. In July he gaily recorded in his diary: 'Mr. Johnson, Dr. Goldsmith, and I supped together at the Mitre . . .', but we can only hazard a guess at how much it pleased him to be able to write so. I do not think this is to exaggerate the importance of Boswell's feeling that he belonged to an inferior race, for even a decade later he can write:

> It was truly satisfactory to me to find myself the only Scotsman among a company of English, and at the time the distinction quite forgotten from our union of interest and from my perfect art of melting myself into the general mass . . .

(Perhaps this entry might also serve to prove that Boswell never drew attention to himself in company by pulling out a notebook and capturing *bon mots* as if they were entomological specimens.)

The end of the London idyll of 1762–3 came when Boswell departed for a year in Utrecht to study law at his father's behest. The studies completed, he won a reward from his father in the shape of a Grand Tour of Europe. He went to Germany, to Switzerland, where he met Voltaire and Rousseau, to Italy, where he met up with Wilkes, to Corsica, to France and, in January 1766, home to Scotland when he read in a Paris newspaper of the death of his mother. His accounts of his journeys, the personalities encountered and incidents which occurred are fascinating. His Corsican journal he turned into a book, published in 1768, which earned him an international reputation. At home in Scotland he began to practise law and continued to find temporary solace in the company of the fair sex.

He had another refuge in times of depression – drink. Up to his mid-twenties, Boswell was a moderate imbiber, but as the years passed, his craving for alcohol increased until he got intoxicated with monotonous regularity. He swore off drink for a year in the spring of 1776 but the resolution could not outlast a month when his actor friend, the great David Garrick, teased him about his abstinence and he succumbed again.

His marriage in 1769 to Margaret Montgomery was the culmination of his search for a wife, which had had slightly comic aspects to it. Margaret was his cousin and she had accompanied him to Dublin where he went with the intention of proposing to a sixteen-year-old Irish heiress called Mary Ann Boyd. Older than he was and more sensible – she it was who said rightly that his diary-keeping would leave him 'embowelled to posterity' – his cousin exerted a steadying influence upon him. He practised law in Edinburgh with a moderate amount of success, but he became ever more prone to sexual and alcoholic excess and to deep black depressions, about which she could do little.

On the other hand, Boswell the diarist and self-analyst could never switch off, even when he felt emotions most people would have preferred to suppress, let alone to recapture and write down for posterity. The death of his small son in 1777 provides a perfect example:

> he expired a little before nine ... I carried the little corpse on my arms up to the drawing-room and laid it on a table covered with a table-cloth, parts of which again I spread over my child. There was something of a dreariness in the blank in our nursery. Yet the gentle death of the sweet innocent, and his appearance like waxwork and at peace after his sufferings, affected us pleasingly ...

And the day after the death:

> I was tenderer today than I imagined, for I cried over my little son and shed many tears. At the same time I had a really pious delight in praying with the room locked, and leaning my hands on his alabaster frame as I knelt ...

Surely only Boswell could truthfully use such words as 'pleasingly' and 'delight' in such circumstances.

There were interludes of euphoria. He made trips to London in 1772 and 1773, seeing his old friends and revisiting old haunts, and in the summer of 1773 had his famous jaunt in the Hebrides with Johnson. The more common situation though was at home in Scotland, subconsciously resenting the fact:

> We had eleven Scotch pints [a Scotch pint equals 3 imperial ones] of claret, two bottles of old hock, and two of port, and drams of brandy and gin . . . I sat after the rest were gone and took a large bowl of admirable soup which did me much good, for I was not sick; though after I was in bed my dear wife was apprehensive that I might die, I breathed so ill . . .
>
> . . . I was, as it were, half boiled with last night's debauch . . .
>
> . . . I drank near three bottles of hock, and then staggered away. I got home about three in the morning . . .
>
> . . . I was still quite giddy with liquor . . .

His depression was sometimes very black:

> *January 24, 1777* . . . I saw death so staringly waiting for all the human race, and had such a cloudy and dark prospect beyond it, that I was miserable as far as I had animation. Either this morning or yesterday I awaked in terrible melancholy . . .
>
> *January 26th, 1778* . . . After dinner took warm port negus to comfort me. Felt universal indifference. This made my wife's death, my own death, anybody's appear of little consequence . . .

and the behaviour sometimes unforgivable:

> *December 8th, 1776* . . . In the evening my wife insisted to read this journal and finding in it such explicit instances of licentiousness, she was much affected . . . [she stayed

only for the sake of the children and for appearances] . . .
At night I calmly meditated to reform . . .

Of course, except in the short term, he could not reform:

January 24, 1778 . . . A little intoxicated. About nine
went out to street. Met fine wench; with her to room in
Blackfriars Wynd, and twice. Back and coffee and
whist . . .

Boswell eventually inherited his father's estate. He made
unsuccessful attempts to enter politics, for his fondest
hope was to enter the House of Commons and live part
of the year in London. He never reached his goal and his
legal career came to a disastrous end when he transferred
to the English bar in 1786. Most of all he wanted to be
neither advocate nor writer but to be recognized as blue-
blooded gentry of ancient lineage. It is one of life's ironies
that many whose lives were the acme of respectability
would have given their right arms to leave an immortal
book behind them, while Boswell, who left an immortal
book, might have offered it in exchange for the
respectability.

By 1789 he was drinking ever more heavily, the butt of
practical jokes and on one occasion the victim of a mugging.
In that year his wife died before he could get to her bedside
from London. His grief was genuine and considerable, but
he would not have been Boswell if the following six years
had not been full of new if unsuccessful matrimonial
schemes. His future executor, Malone, prodded and pushed
him throughout these years of political and private schemes,
and as a result, on 16 May 1791, the twenty-eighth anni-
versary of the first meeting of biographer and subject, *The
Life of Samuel Johnson, LL.D.* ('exhibiting a view of literature and literary men in Great Britain, for near half a century, during which he flourished'), was published never to
lapse out of print again.

His wife would not have been particularly impressed.

When the tour with Johnson was mooted, her reaction was that she had heard of a man leading a bear, but a bear leading a man was ridiculous. Perhaps now, if she but knew how highly her husband's portrait in depth has since been regarded, and how exciting we find the diary that so shocked her in her lifetime, she might change her mind.

BIBLIOGRAPHY

James Boswell: The Yale Editions of the Private Papers of James Boswell (published in Britain by Heinemann). The following volumes are of particular interest: *Boswell's London Journal 1762–3*, 1950 (also published as a Penguin Book, number 2538, in 1966); *Boswell on the Grand Tour 1764* (Germany and Switzerland), 1953; *Boswell on the Grand Tour 1765–66* (Italy, Corsica and France), 1955; *Boswell in Search of a Wife 1766–69*, 1957; *Boswell for the Defence 1769–1774*, 1960; *Boswell: the Ominous Years 1774–76*, 1963; *Boswell in Extremes 1776–78*, 1971.

Frederick A. Pottle: *James Boswell: the Earlier Years 1740–69* (Heinemann, 1966).

SIX

The Diarist in Society

The diaries of famous men and women seem obvious places for an historian to ferret out impressions of social importance. Man, after all, is a gregarious creature, and the well known, many perhaps with a greater sense of self-importance, could be expected to have a nose for the significant, even if it occurs only within their own social circle. But the diary, even for the most journalistic minds, is more than a mere record of events: to some a confidential friend, to others an outlet for frustrations, the diary is so prone to emotion and personal bias as to be completely useless as an impartial witness to social events. Moreover, famous men and women, notwithstanding their own personal success, seem just as prone to short-sightedness and misjudgment as their more anonymous compatriots in the street.

Man's inability to judge the present by the future's standards does not negate the value of the diary to anyone interested in looking at life in times past. However, the most interesting perceptions about society are often to be found in the most unlikely diaries, in the words of people whose fame rests solely on their daily entries. And it is precisely in those entries written hastily or without a great amount of thought because of their contemporary unimportance that the most interesting discoveries about society can be made by the present-day reader.

Wading through a great sea of words for one interesting passage can hardly be enjoyable to anyone but the most dedicated historian. To be of interest to the general reader, the social diary must contain more than one unconscious piece of social evidence, and the diarist's entries should reflect his own life as well as the world around him. He need not be famous, though connections and friendships with the more noteworthy may serve to widen his own experiences and make him more cognisant of the changes in whatever social world he frequents. But the most important qualifications of the great social diarist are curiosity and an uncontrollable desire to record whatever his perceptive mind sees of interest, however slight. In the diary of such a writer one can find double delight in the revelations of his daily life and in the satisfying discovery of a piece of social history.

The seventeenth-century diary of Elias Ashmole, for example, reflects the contemporary preoccupation with the mysteries of natural science. Ashmole's interest in astrology, his careful analysis of all his own diseases and their symptoms, and his collection of scientific 'rarities', are three aspects of the way in which seventeenth-century man tried to interpret natural laws and attempted to understand the world about him. Ashmole, unlike many of his time, does not look upon religion as the explanation of the natural world, but seeks concrete revelations of the laws of nature. His curiosity was to our ultimate benefit, for he is credited with having established the first museum of natural history in Britain when he gave his personal collection of natural curiosities to Oxford University. (The Ashmolean Museum at Oxford still retains his name, although much of the original collection is now elsewhere.)

Ashmole was born on 23 May 1617, the only son of Thomas Ashmole of Lichfield, a saddler whose sole claim to fame was that he twice became chief bailiff for that city. Ashmole was not content to follow in his father's undistinguished footsteps and some regard him as something of a social climber. Through his own resources and a series of judicious marriages (aided no doubt by the high mortality rate of those days), he achieved a certain prominence, including an appointment in 1660 by King Charles II as Comptroller of the Excise and Windsor Herald. His talents included alchemy, astrology, fortune-telling, healing and heraldry, and his acquaintance ranged from royalty to most of the important scientific figures of the time.

Ashmole's first step up the ladder of success was provided by his cousin, Thomas Pagit. Impressed with young Ashmole's talents, Pagit arranged for him to be sent to the Lichfield Grammar School (the school that produced Dr Johnson, Addison and David Garrick). From there he became a chorister in the Cathedral School. In a world where learning was a luxury, such an education gave him a head start.

In 1637, Ashmole decided to cap his educational advantage with a judicious marriage to Elianor Mainwaring, eldest daughter of Mr Peter Mainwaring. His cryptic entries for 1637 indicate a certain lack of initial success:

> *Aug. 21.* I came to Smalewood, to Mr. Peter Mainwaring's, to ask his consent to marry his daughter.
> *Sept. 4.* The second time I went to Smalewood.
> *Sept. 16.* I returned to London.

Ashmole was not discouraged by this initial rebuff, and his perseverance paid off when he duly married Elianor in 1638. It was a short-lived marriage, for in 1641 Elianor took ill of a fever and died. Determined not to relinquish his newly-won family connections with the Mainwarings, in 1649 he married Lady Mainwaring of a yet more prosperous branch of the family. He records in his diary the many presents the good lady gave him before the nuptials were celebrated.

Marital bliss was not the only concern of young Ashmole during the period. He was already cementing important connections and writing the first of his many works on astrology. His diary is full of entries concerning the 'Astrologer's Feasts' he attended, and his own reliance on the methods of the 'science'. Following one such banquet in 1651, he records a cure brought about by astrological methods.

Aug. 14, 1651 The Astrologers' Feast at Painters Hall, London.

This night about one a'clock, I feel ill of a surfeit, occasioned by drinking water after venison. I was greatly oppressed in my stomach; and next day Mr. Saunders the astrologian sent me a piece of bryony root to hold my hand, and within a quarter of an hour, my stomach was freed of that great oppression, which nothing which I took from Dr. Wharton could do before.

Astrology was but one of the manifestations of the perplexities that dominated seventeenth-century life. The age was filled with religious and political strife, and although Ashmole's diary makes no mention of the English Civil War in the 1640s, his entries show the many ways in which people sought to explain the troubled times in which they were living. Witches were still believed to be agents of the Devil and in August 1652, Ashmole went to the Maidstone Assizes to hear the trials of some supposed witches.

Other people sought to explain the political and religious confusion as an indication of the Second Coming. Prophets were common, preaching the end of the world or the coming of Christ. One such prophet was a Welshman, Arise Evans, who declared himself to be Christ in 1647. Ashmole met him in 1653, and while not completely believing the would-be Christ, his own faith in the supernatural made him less than sceptical of the powers of such men.

This morning I first became acquainted with Arise Evans, a Welsh prophet; and speaking of the Parliament, I asked him when it would end? He answered, the time was short, and it was even at the door; this very morning at eleven a'clock, the Mace was taken away from the Speaker, and the Parliament was dissolved; and I conjecture it was much about the time that Arise Evans and I had this discourse.

While Ashmole took this great interest in astrology and

prophets, his interest in more conventional subjects had not lagged. In 1658 he began two projects – a history of the Order of the Garter, and a description of the coins which he found in the Oxford archives. His appointment as Windsor Herald by the King in 1660 brought him to Court, where he quickly made a name for himself if only for his penchant for displaying his collection of natural curiosities and specimens to anyone prepared to provide an audience. Among the rather grisly samples he showed the King were a four-month-old foetus and a pair of Siamese twins.

> *Oct. 12, 1660.* This morning I showed the King the young children which Dr. Warner had preserved. The one was a male infant about 4 months, who was cut out of a woman's belly in Covent Garden (she dying of a consumption) and had been (now four years past) luted up in a glass, and preserved by a liquor of his preparation from putrefaccon, the flesh not so much as rumpled, but plump as it was when taken out of the wombe. The other was 2 girls joyned together by the breast and belly (which monster was borned about the king's coming in), they were dryed, and preserved with spices.

Despite Ashmole's interest in the rational world, the appearance of Siamese twins was still looked upon as a supernatural omen.

Over the next six years, Ashmole continued his researches and collections of specimens. In 1666, he presented to the Library at Oxford three folio volumes containing a description of the 'consular and imperial coines there' written painstakingly in his own hand; he took particular pride in the inscription which was entered in the register of benefactors informing all posterity of his gift. His happiness at the completion of such a work was perhaps slightly marred by the death of Lady Mainwaring in 1668, but Ashmole soon recovered (he had been on strained terms with his wife) and he married for the third time, to one Mrs Elizabeth Dugdale, in the same year.

In 1672, Ashmole completed what he thought was his greatest achievement, his *History of the Order and Institution of the Garter*, which was indeed a success, especially in Court circles.

> The Earl of Peterborough having about June, by the Duke of York's command, called at my Chambers, in the Temple, for one of my Books of the Garter, to carry to the Duke, then at sea; he this day told me the Duke received it with much pleasure, and (the Earl) believed he had read it all over.

Ashmole must have felt an author's pride at not only having his book owned, but actually read and appreciated by the people he most wanted to impress.

In 1693, Ashmole began to send his curiosities to Oxford to the original Ashmolean Museum which was built to house them. His beloved 'Rarietes' had found a home of intellectual distinction which would be a continuing tribute to their curious collector. Ashmole himself died in 1693, after a full and successful life. His diaries, which are full of his illnesses, his 'pocks', 'sweats' and cures, nevertheless tell the story of an intellectually healthy man searching for the truth about natural phenomena in an age too often misguided by portents and superstitions.

Mary, Countess Cowper and Lady of the Bedchamber to the Princess of Wales, also used marriage as a rung on the social ladder. She was born Mary Clavering in 1685, the daughter of John Clavering Esquire of Chopwell in Durham. She met her future husband, William, Lord Cowper, over some law business in London and married him in 1706. The marriage had to be kept a secret for a while, because of the disapproval of his mother (to whom Mary was later reconciled). Lord Cowper was a very good catch for the young country girl. At the time of his marriage he was Lord Keeper of the Great Seal and he

was afterwards to become Lord Chancellor. Rather a ladies'
man, he had Lady Harriet de Vere chasing him until the
minute his marriage was made known: Lady Harriet would
have stopped at nothing to win him, and had even warned
him that Mary was a young woman of easy virtue.

If Lord Cowper was the catch of the season, then in
young Mary he had found his equal. She was charming,
well-read and well educated, and translated her husband's
memoirs into French so they could be read by the mostly
non-English-speaking Hanoverian Court. Her beauty and
affability were an asset to any gentleman seeking a position
in the royal court, and her discrimination and intelligence
kept them safer than most amidst the intrigue and gossip so
common at the time.

Mary had always been a Whig and in favour of the
Hanoverian succession. In the years before her diary was
written, she had been an intimate correspondent of
Catherine of Anspach who was married to the would-be
Prince of Wales. When Queen Anne died and George I
was crowned in 1714, Caroline came to Court with the
rest of the Hanoverian entourage, and Mary, not un-
naturally, expected a place with her. After initial delay
and uncertainty, she was made Lady of the Bedchamber
and began a diary about her experiences at Court. Her
diary is in two parts, the first covering October 1714 to
October 1716, and the second the year of 1720. In the
first part, Mary describes the Jacobite Rebellion of 1715,
when the Pretender attempted to regain the English crown,
and in the second she discusses the reconciliation between
King George I and the Prince of Wales, who had been
quarrelling for some years.

In 1714, the English Court was full of intrigue and
political squabbles, most of which continued far into the
century. The Hanoverian succession was, as yet, by no
means certain, and there were many in the country who
supported 'James III' who planned to return to England
and claim the throne. (Son of the late King, James II, he

had been expelled to France along with his father in the Glorious Revolution of 1688.) Rumours about the Pretender's whereabouts, coupled with the usual contradictory Court gossip, stimulated Mary to write down her own impressions and make some record of the truth for herself.

> The perpetual Lies that One hears have determined me, in spite of my Want of Leisure, to write down all the Events that are worth remembering whilst I am at *Court*; and although I find it will be impossible for me to do this daily, yet I hope I shall be able to have an Hour or two once a Week: and I intend this only for my own Use, it being a rought Draft only, which, if *God* bless me with Health and Leisure, I intend hereafter to revise and digest into a better method.

While Mary's diary touches on the important political events of the time, as might be expected in a Court diary, it is also full of information about the London of the early eighteenth century, a much smaller city than we know now, in every sense. Imagine a time when Bloomsbury was the home of the aristocracy, and open fields stretched from there to Hampstead:

> *Nov. 30, 1714.* This Day was employed in packing, for removing from *Russell Street* (where I had a delightful House, with the finest view backwards of any House in Town) to the House in *Lincoln's Inn Fields* . . .

In Mary's London, the theatre was one of the few evening diversions for the Court. In spite of the great differences between Restoration theatre and the theatre of today (women had started to appear for the first time on the stage only in the 1660s), obscenity on the stage was as burning an issue then as it is now. Mary seems to have had more discrimination than many of her fellow playgoers and, much to her satisfaction, she was able to convince the Princess that the current offering, *The Wanton Wife*

or *The Amorous Widow*, was no more obscene than any other
comedy produced at the time.

> Went to the Play with my Mistress; and, to my great
> Satisfaction, she liked it as well as any Play she had
> seen; and it certainly is not more obscene than all
> Comedies are. It were to be wished our Stage was chaster;
> and I cannot hope, now it is under Mr. *Steele's* Direction,
> that it will mend.

Sir Richard Steele had recently been appointed the governor
of the Drury Lane Theatre, mostly because it was believed
he would ensure a healthy legitimate theatre. Once in
nominal charge, he was content to concentrate on his
political career instead.

Fortunately, Mary had as little time to devote to the
reform of the theatre as Sir Richard. Life at Court was
extremely busy and tiring. Along with her own tasks, she
had to contend with troublesome relatives, all wanting to
take advantage of her position near the King and Queen.
Mary had the sense and ability to keep her less capable
relations well out of sight.

> *Dec. 14, 1714.* Mrs. *Tuttle* came to see me in the Morning.
> She told me that my Relations took it ill of me that I
> did not go oftener to them; and that my Aunt expected
> I should have got her a Place about the *Princess*, and my
> Uncle another in the *Salt Office*. How People judge of
> their own Merit!

Meddling relatives were but one of the problems that
Mary had to contend with, meanwhile keeping her temper.
When George I ascended to the throne, he brought many
foreign ladies to the Court. Some of these ladies brought
grace and manners with them, but others, feeling insecure
and unwelcome in London, sought every opportunity to
denigrate the English and showed bad manners when in
society. A particular thorn in Mary's flesh was Mademoiselle
Schutz who went out of her way to pester her. Mary had

4

the manners and good sense not to insult the Mademoiselle openly, but she must have taken vicarious pleasure when Lady Deloraine struck a blow for the English in getting the better of the Countess of Buckenburgh.

> Countess of Buckenburgh said, in a Visit, that the English Women did not look like Women of Quality, but made themselves look as pitifully and sneakingly as they could; that they hold their heads down, and look always in a Fright, whereas those that are Foreigners hold up their Heads and hold out their Breasts, and make themselves look as great and stately as they can, and more nobly and more like Quality than the others. To which Lady Deloraine replied, 'We show our Quality by our Birth and Titles, Madam, and not by sticking out our Bosoms!!'

Lady Cowper's diary also shows her interest in the public events taking place during her years at Court. She records the rise of Sir Robert Walpole as first minister to the King, though she did not much like his influence over the Princess, and also the over-speculation in the South Sea Company which caused the South Sea Bubble to burst in 1720. She had little sympathy for those who had invested heavily in the scheme. She casts doubts on the supposed reconciliation between George I and his son in 1720, noting that the King refused to speak to his son during the time of supposed new harmony, and is affronted when she and other friends of the Prince and Princess are treated disrespectfully on their return to the King's Court, after their few years in 'exile' caused by the rupture between father and son.

One feeling that remained constant through the turmoil was Mary's affection for her husband. When he fell ill, her thoughts were continually with him, and she considered giving up her life at Court, if peace and quiet in the country could make him well. She would even share poverty with him.

Feb. 16, 1716. I am out of my Wits to see him suffer, which I declare is ten Times worse than Death to me, and would rather live with him all my Life on Bread and Cheese, up three Pair of Stairs, than be all this World can make me and at the same time see him suffer.

The sentiments may seem naïve and the vision of poverty essentially romantic, but Lady Mary Cowper lasted a scant six months after the death of her husband in 1723, and reports suggest she died of a broken heart. Her journals survive to show us an intelligent and lively woman, casting an original and unusual light on the early Hanoverian Court.

The next hundred years brought great changes to English life. The agricultural revolution improved farming, both in quality and quantity, and the new canals made it easier to ship goods to the growing cities. The faint rumblings of the coming Industrial Revolution could be heard as inventions like the spinning jenny encouraged the growth of factories which in turn brought workers streaming into the towns from the countryside. English 'Society' had also changed. It had become more mannered, more refined in its own eyes and more selective in its company. Yet there was still room for an outsider to climb into its ranks, just as Elias Ashmole had done over 150 years before.

Thomas Moore, the son of a Dublin grocer, achieved a place in London society through his popular poems and lyrics. He was lucky in being able to profit by the Acts of 1793 which removed many of the civil restrictions for Catholics in Ireland, and he became a law student. In 1799, Moore felt the time was ripe to leave Dublin and to conquer London. During his first visit he composed his *Odes of Anacreon* which caused a stir in the *Edinburgh Review*. He returned to Dublin, but not for long, because he had decided to make London his home. In 1801, a book of lyrics coupled with his earlier *Odes* brought him not only fame but influential patronage and an entrée into smart London society. Moore did not use marriage as a step up the social ladder, for in 1811 he married a young actress, Bessy Dykes, to whom he was devoted for the rest of his life. Instead, he relied on the success of his *Irish Melodies* (1807) and an oriental romance, *Lalla Rookh* (1817), to earn him the esteem of those he most wished to impress.

Moore's other claim to fame (for certainly his poems did not much outlast his lifetime) was his friendship with the considerably more illustrious poet, Byron. He and Moore were very close friends and Moore watched with sadness the disintegration of the great poet's life. Byron, shortly before his death, gave his memoirs to Moore, who intended to steer them through publication. After the poet's death, the Byron family opposed publication. Moore, in an act of appeasement history finds hard to forgive, handed the precious manuscript to Byron's executors who promptly destroyed it. Fortunately for posterity, Moore kept some of Byron's letters and journals which he published in 1829 under the title of *Letters and Journals of Lord Byron*. He is also remembered for a biography of Sheridan published in 1825.

Moore's journal, which runs from 1818 to 1841, is in large part a tribute to himself. He swells with pride in having such social connections as Lord and Lady Holland and other members of the aristocracy, and can hardly wait to record the times he is to spend in their company. Although he writes too of his devotion to his wife Bessy and his children, they rarely appear to take any part in his social life, but are kept more or less cloistered in their country cottage lest they interfere with the busy poet's London activities.

Moore was also extremely pleased with his own personal success. He enjoyed the adulation of the public and its concomitant, being recognized in shops and theatres. He also enjoyed receiving fan mail from his readers, and although he pretended to be annoyed at the various requests he received from would-be authors, he was secretly pleased at their adulation.

Aug 24, 1818. Arrived at my cottage. Always glad to return to it, and the dear girl who makes it so happy for me. Found heaps of letters, some of them from poets and authors, who are the pest of my life; – one sending me a 'Serio-comic Drama of Invasion, in Three Acts, including the Vision and the Battle' and referring me for his poetic credentials to three admirals and 'the late comptroller of the navy'! Another begging to know whether I was acquainted with 'any man or woman to whom money was for a time useless', who would venture £100 upon a literary speculation he had in hand. The third letter from an eternal Amelia Louisa, announcing to me that her long threatened MS. was on its way to Wiltshire for my perusal.

Unfortunately Moore's enjoyment of his own fame and the London high-life was interrupted by a short sojourn abroad, when he was forced to flee London to escape financial difficulties occasioned by the default of a deputy which left him liable for £6,000. His travels, which included a meeting with his friend Byron in Italy, show the continuing interest of English travellers in the beauties of Europe. It had only been in the latter part of the eighteenth century that the 'Grand Tour' of Europe had become obligatory for a well-educated gentleman, so by Moore's time Englishmen were still only just becoming aware of European natural and man-made wonders. Moore's first view of the Alps and his reaction to it must have been an experience common to many wealthy young Englishmen – notably Wordsworth.

September 27, 1819. That mighty panorama of the Alps, whose summits there, indistinctly seen, looked like the top of gigantic waves, following close upon each other; the soft lights falling on those green spots which cultivation has conjured up in the midst of this wild scene;

the pointed top of the Jungfrau, whose snows were then pink with the setting sun; all was magnificent to a degree that quite overpowered me, and I alternately shuddered and shed tears as I looked upon it.

The £6,000 debt was paid by 1822 and once back in London Moore continued his round of social engagements and his own writing. As a final social coup, he was invited to a party where Princess Augusta, the sister of King George IV, entertained the assembled guests by singing. His joy was only slightly dimmed by his own regret at handing the Byron memoirs over to Byron's executors. He is able to rationalize that decision on hearing of a conversation of Byron's from a friend.

We then sat down to the luncheon; and it was quite amusing to find how much at my ease I felt myself; having consorted with princes in my time, but not knowing much of the female gender of royalty. I ought to have mentioned that in the course of my conversations these two days past with Hobhouse, he frequently stated that, having remonstrated with Lord Byron the last time he saw him on the impropriety of putting a document of the nature of these memoirs out of his own power, Lord B. had expressed regret at having done so, and alleged considerations of delicacy towards me as his only reason for not recalling them. This, if I wanted any justification to myself for what I have done, would abundantly satisfy me as to the propriety of the sacrifice.

Moore's own popularity made easier meetings with other literary personalities of the time. A letter to Sir Walter Scott brought him an invitation to stay with the writer at his home in Scotland. Moore got along very well with Scott, and the great romantic writer confided one source of his plots.

Aug. 29, 1825. Had always been in the habit (while

wandering or shooting) of forming stories and following a train of adventures in his mind, and these fancies it was that formed the ground-work of most of his novels.

Writers were not the only V.I.P.s that Moore met. At a dinner the famous actress, Mrs Sarah Siddons, who had by then retired from the stage, confided her secret for great acting:

Among other reasons for her regret at leaving the stage was, that she always found in it a vent for her private sorrows, which enabled her to bear them better; and often she has got credit for the truth and feeling of her acting when she was doing nothing more than relieving her own heart of its grief.

Thomas Moore's diary is a selective look at upper-class English Regency society through the eyes of a social climber. Thanks to his being an outsider, aspiring to the highest social ranks, Moore is more observant of those he wishes to emulate and his diary is more informative because of this than it might otherwise have been. His constant name-dropping and lists of the social gatherings he attended become wearying after a while, and one can only have pity for poor Bessy, isolated in her country cottage, who had to hear all the tiresome details first hand.

Sir William Hardman was also a self-conscious diarist. His diaries were originally in the form of letters to Edward Holroyd, a good friend practising law in Australia, but he preserved a copy of every letter in bound volumes, conscious of their value for future generations.

Born on 13 August 1838, the son of William Bridge Hardman, William Hardman was educated at the Bury Grammar School and Trinity College, Cambridge where he took his degree in 1850. He decided to read law and was called to the Bar at the Inner Temple in 1852. Ambitions to enter national politics proved futile, but he turned to journalism and participated in politics at a local level. From 1865 until his death in 1890 he was Chairman of the Surrey Quarter Session, services for which he was knighted in 1885. He also became Mayor of Kingston-on-Thames in 1870, and from 1872 onward was editor of *The Morning Post*. He married Mary Anne Radley in 1855 and had two daughters to whom he was devoted.

Hardman has been described by one of his editors, S. M. Ellis, as a 'mid-Victorian Pepys'. This appellation is ridiculously ambitious, for Hardman has none of Pepys's humour or honesty of vision nor his wide circle of acquaintance. Yet, in a limited way, Hardman's diaries do give something of the flavour of mid-Victorian England. Writing from 1859 to August 1871, Hardman records many of the political and social changes during this time, and his intimate friendship with George Meredith, the poet and novelist, gained him an entrée into literary circles. Instead of the fearless Pepys, whose diary entries tell us everything, Hardman is more circumspect, an ardent Tory whose gossip is more often merely a confirmation of his own opinions.

Not long after William Hardman began his diary, the American Civil War broke out. This event was more serious for many Englishmen than is often realized, for the Southern States supplied many of the English factories with raw cotton. If the North had prevented the Southern supply of cotton from reaching England, it would have meant serious financial difficulties for the factory owners and their employees. Hardman, like many English colleagues, was on the Southern side, despite the fact that the Southern plantation owners still kept slaves. Compounded with Hardman's initial dislike of the Northerners was what he felt was an indifferent reception of the Prince of Wales during his trip to the United States in 1860, to smooth the strained relations between the North and England. Although war between England and the North was averted, Hardman was still suspicious of Yankee motives.

We are the last people who could undertake the mediation between the contending parties: we are viewed with too much suspicion and hatred. I am much inclined to the opinion that if the Northerners are successful, they will make an onslaught on Canada. Truly we have fallen upon warlike times, and we yet see but faintly and amid glimmering obscurity the ultimate issues of this great American contest.

If Hardman had contempt for the North ('the Yankees are a damned lot, and republican institutions are all rot'), he had nothing but admiration for the Prince of Wales and his conduct during the negotiations. Edward, Prince of Wales was an admirable foreign diplomat when he became King Edward VII; though Hardman's criteria for a successful monarch were of a different category:

October, 1860. In point of fact, our future sovereign possesses two great qualifications for an English king: he is a first-rate horseman and a crack shot; and with it the hearty qualities of a hunter and sportsman generally, he combines sound common sense and quiet, gentlemanly demeanour, with a taste for literature and the fine arts, he will be as great an ornament to the throne of this country as his excellent mother.

When Hardman was not discoursing on the intricacies of political and royal life, he was a keen gourmet and avid conversationalist, common qualifications for a diarist. He and his wife Mary-Anne gave many dinner parties, and at one, contrary to the prevailing Victorian code, smoking was allowed in front of the ladies. Hardman's friendship with George Meredith brought him into contact with other literary notables, whose company and conversation he much enjoyed. To celebrate his friendship with some of these people, he gave a special dinner at his club one evening.

April, 1862. I had a very select dinner-party at the Club

4*

last night. Meredith, Dante Rossetti, and Dr. Liveing
were my part, and I flatter myself they never sat down
to a better selected meal in their lives. They were enthusiastic, and I have added fresh laurels to my fame as
a dinner giver. An enviable notoriety, but expensive.
The following was the dinner:

MENU	*Wine*
Oysters, bearded, brown bread and butter	
Côtelettes de saumon à l'indienne	Chablis
Filets de boeuf grillés au beurre d'anchois	
Épinards au jus	Amontillado
Côtelettes d'agneau à l'italienne	
Fricassée de poulet à la Marengo	Sparkling hock
Choux-fleurs au gratin	
Omelette aux fraises	
Maccaroni au gratin	

> Wine after dinner: Chambertin.
> Coffee: Dry curaçao.
> Cigars: *ad libitum*.

Among the other diversions which entertained Hardman
and his family was the theatre. Mid-nineteenth-century
theatre had none of the refinement introduced at the end
of the century. Theatres were uncomfortable, smelly and
ill-lit. Often, as Hardman notes, the show in the audience
was more entertaining than the staged performance. Still,
the theatre was one of the few live entertainments available,
and the Drury Lane Theatre as popular then as it is now,
if a trifle more rowdy:

December, 1862. We went to Drury Lane on Boxing
Night, and such a pandemonium I have rarely witnessed.
The first piece was acted in dumb show, not a word
could we hear. The fights in pit and gallery were frequent.
The shower of orange peel from the gods into the pit

was quite astounding. The occupants of the latter place made feeble efforts to throw it back again, but, of course, never got it any further than the first tier of boxes. I was glad to see the thing once, but you won't catch me there again . . .

Many middle-class families regarded the theatre as a place of disrepute and a den of iniquity – perhaps quite justly.

During Hardman's lifetime the city of London changed into a real metropolis. As it expanded, travel from one part of the city to another became more and more difficult. To solve the problem, railways were constructed, connecting the various parts of London. By the 1860s some of the lines had gone underground, and Mr Hardman was curious enough to take a trip on the 'Drain'.

Monday, 26th (January), 1863. Yesterday Mary Ann and I made our first trip down the 'Drain'. We walked to the Edgware Road and took first class tickets for King's Cross (6d. each). We experienced no disagreeable odour, beyond the smell common to tunnels. The carriages hold ten persons, with divided seats, and are lighted by gas (two lights), they are so lofty that a six footer may stand erect with his hat on. Trains run every 15 minutes from six in the morning till twelve at night (with some slight variation), and about 30,000 are conveyed on the line daily: shares have risen, and there is a prospect of a large dividend.

(The service sounds better than today's!) Hardman's experience is indicative of the change the Underground system made to London. The suburbs boomed and the one-time necessity that a man live near his place of business was gone for ever. Hardman was not particularly aware of the implications of the changes which he noted in his diary, but with the benefit of hindsight we can glean an interesting contrast between his world and our own.

Lady Frederick Cavendish lived at the same time as

William Hardman, but in a completely different world. Lady Frederick was born Lucy Caroline Lyttelton, the second daughter and second child of George William, the fourth Lord Lyttelton by his first wife Mary. Lady Lyttelton went on to have ten more children, so that Lucy grew up in the midst of a large, genial and well-connected family. Lord Lyttelton's mother was Lady Sarah Spencer who between 1842 and 1850 was the supervisor of the Royal school-rooms and was called by some the 'Governess of England'. Lucy's aunt, Lady Lyttelton's sister, was married to W. H. Gladstone, a relation which would serve Lucy's future husband well.

Lucy's childhood was chiefly spent at Hagley, her father's house in Worcestershire. She had a typical Victorian childhood with perhaps more emphasis on cricket and the Church than was usual. That religion became an important part of her life is reflected in her diary. In 1857, Lady Lyttelton died leaving Meriel, the eldest daughter, in charge of the family, but on Meriel's marriage in 1859 Lucy herself became surrogate mother to her brothers and sisters.

The maternal duties ceased in 1863 when Lucy became a Maid of Honour to Queen Victoria. Before she could tire of her duties, she became engaged to Lord Frederick Cavendish, the second son of the Duke of Devonshire. They married in June 1864, and their life together was marred only by the fact that they had no children.

The marriage stimulated Lucy's interest in politics, for her husband entered Parliament as a Liberal in July 1865. A poor speaker, but an earnest party man, his loyalty was eventually rewarded in 1882 when he was made Chief Secretary for Ireland. After a few tragic days in office, he was tragically assassinated, though his wife was to live on until 1925.

Her diaries extend over a period of twenty-eight years from 1854, when she was thirteen, until the murder of her husband in 1882. The diaries are much more than the idle

reminiscences of a young society lady. Lucy's social conscience had made her aware of those less fortunate than herself from an early age. She lived through one of the many
cholera epidemics of the nineteenth century (before the
disease was known to be water-borne), and outlined what
devastation the death of the head of the family could cause
an unprotected widow.

> *Hagley, September 6, 1854.* The cholera is fearful in
> London; more than 1,000–200 [*sic*] fatal cases. Four
> children in one family. A poor clergyman caught the
> typhus fever from one of his sons, and his wife was
> confined with an eighth baby while he was so ill. She
> recovered to find herself a widow with eight children,
> and not a farthing to support herself or them; his living
> having been given away, and so no money from thence,
> he hadn't insured his life, and had no fortune besides.
> They are collecting money. I gave a little, and Albert.
> They have already collected a great deal, and have taken
> three children off her hands.

Throughout her life she continued to be as concerned about
the plight of the poor and unfortunate. In 1866 she notes
in her diary the setting up of a London soup kitchen (on
Liberal principles, of course).

> *London, February 13, 1866.* Poor people (not beggars)
> are given tickets, on showing which and paying a sum
> not exceeding 2d. they get good meat, soup, beef-tea, or
> pudding of at least twice the value of what they pay.

A bargain indeed for those who possessed the necessary 2d.!
A well-educated Victorian lady was expected to be
interested in other things besides the plight of the poor.
On her many trips to London, young Lucy went the
rounds of various exhibitions, including the galleries. Her
comments on the new Pre-Raphaelite paintings of such men
as Ford Madox Brown and Holman Hunt echo many of the
art critics of the time.

London, May 30th, 1859. In the morning we went to the
Exhibition, where there are not many beautiful pictures,
and a host of glaring absurd Pre-Raphaelites, with every
face bright pink, and every sky of lilac, tin leaves and
grass like coarse stuffs, and a lunatic attempt to render
every atom as it *is*, instead of as it looks. The result is
like the sign of an inn; a laboured and vulgar finish,
with a dazzle of ill-assorted colours. Pah! the refinement
of turning to Stanfields fresh and living landscapes with
soft blending light, and *wet* water.

William Hardman's dinner guest Dante Rossetti, one of the
most eminent Pre-Raphaelites, would hardly have taken
kindly to so severe a verdict on his work.

Lucy Cavendish and William Hardman were more at
one on the subject of the American Civil War. Like her
fellow Victorian, Lucy was on the side of the South and
thought the Americans as disagreeable as did Hardman.

London, Tuesday, June 2nd, 1863. I sat next an exceedingly
agreeable Mr. Bourke, who has seen a good deal of
America. He said the people were quite as hateful as
books describe them. And he told me of one horrible
thing: they dare to push their democracy into their very
ideas of Heaven; i.e. they will never give to the Almighty
the title of 'King of Kings', or any other which implies
sovereign authority, as being contrary to their notions of
universal equality!!

To the Victorian English mind, republicanism in any form
verged on blasphemy.

Lady Frederick's diaries also deal with Court life during
the Victorian years. She describes the grand 'Drawing-
Rooms' before the Prince Consort's death in 1861 and the
dances and magnificent suppers. After the death of her
husband, austerity was the keynote of Queen Victoria's
receptions. Only after the marriage of Prince Edward to
Princess Alexandra of Denmark was there a new centre

for aristocratic conviviality. When Lucy came to Windsor in 1863 to become a Maid of Honour, it was a subdued Court she entered, with the Queen still in mourning.

She confided her nervousness to her diary:

September 11, 1863. Oh dear, I shall sympathize for the rest of my life with poor peggies [maidservants] launched at their first place! To-day has taught me what it is to 'feel strange'.

Actually, Lucy did well at Court and the Queen was sorry to see her leave on her marriage to Frederick Cavendish. Lucy's farewell to the Queen shows her deep affection for the monarch and also the Queen's deep personal suffering for her lost Albert.

Windsor, Friday, May 13th, 1864. After luncheon the Queen sent for me to say good-bye, and I hope I shall never forget what passed. She came towards me with many kind words about her regret that I was going, and her good wishes for me. She kissed me again and again, saying she thought and felt the more for me because I had no mother. The ornament she gave me was a beautiful amethyst locket bordered with pearls; on it a little diamond cross. Speaking of the cross, she said, 'It is an emblem of what I have to bear day after day,' . . .

Leaving the maudlin Queen, Lucy and her husband left on a grand European tour.

Martigny, Thursday, July 7th, 1864. Got into a bus at Martigny crammed with English folk, but they don't seem to overrun this hotel. Why does one hate and despise nearly all one's fellow country-men abroad?

Lady Frederick Cavendish and William Hardman frequented different Victorian worlds, but in both their diaries the essential self-satisfied complacency of the middle and upper classes shines through. Theirs was a world getting better every day and one which would soon, in spite of underlying problems, become the best of all possible worlds – for some.

Disillusionment with Victorian ideals was part of the Edwardian ethos. It became clear to intellectual and non-intellectual alike that things were not going to get better overnight. In fact, there was the possibility (to some people the certainty) that society was too rotten ever to reform itself. Disillusionment with Victorian standards was shown most clearly in the arts. Plays which challenged the social norm, novels which investigated behavioural motivation, and paintings which rejected Victorian visual sentimentality all contributed to a general awareness that the complacent Victorian life could not continue unaltered. The artist, writer, playwright, or painter was perhaps most sensitive to these changes, whether he merely observed or participated in explaining them.

Charles De Sousy Ricketts was an artist who took advantage of the late-Victorian revolution in the visual arts to work as painter, printer, stage-designer, writer and collector, a varied career which he recorded in his diaries. He was born on 2 October 1866, the son of a Naval Officer and a French mother. His art training began at sixteen when he was apprenticed to a wood-engraver at the City and Guilds Technical Art School in London. It was here that he met C. H. Shannon, with whom he later lived and worked.

Inheriting £500 from his grandfather, Ricketts put into practice his ideas, taken largely from William Morris, of the artist as a total craftsman. Ricketts took the Master's ideas to heart and set up the Vale Press (1896–1904) for which he designed founts, papers and bindings. He and his friend Shannon also set up *The Dial* (1889–97), a periodical devoted to literature and painting, and the pair also worked together on prints.

In 1904 Ricketts gave up printing to devote himself

more to painting and occasional modelling. In 1906, influenced by Leon Bakst, he also took to stage design. Like Bakst, he believed that one colour should predominate a stage set and that a large pattern rightly placed could be particularly effective on the stage. He designed the sets and costumes for productions of Shaw's *Saint Joan* in 1924 and Wilde's *Salome* in 1906, though his best work is thought to be for a 1925 production of *Henry VIII*.

Ricketts' paintings got him elected to the Royal Academy in 1928, but perhaps his greatest service to British Art was the collection of old masters, Japanese and Greek prints and drawing and *objets d'art* which he and Shannon eventually donated to the public. Though neither Ricketts nor Shannon was particularly well off during their lifetime, they continued to buy works of art that interested them and which they could afford. Today the collection would be virtually priceless.

Ricketts was excited by the work of the many talented poets, playwrights and musicians working at the turn of the century, but, for the most part, out of sympathy with the artists of his time. Some attributed this distaste to his abhorrence of opaque paint, though one suspects this is a minor factor. Despite his dislike of Post-Impressionism and the new school of English artists, what he felt was much worse was the total lack of artistic discernment he found in England. The English, he felt, could not see the painting for the clever brush-work.

July 11, 1900. He (Shannon) said what is perfectly true, that the most ignorant Frenchman believes Art to be Art, in some sense admirable or useful, however base his taste; that in England a few only rise above the smallest matters of fact; they note in a picture the polish on the boots, or the signs of wear on a man's sleeve; the art of a thing, the fact that Art is Art, never touches them.

This inability to see the whole, or in the famous words of another Edwardian, E. M. Forster, to 'only connect', extended beyond the realm of art. Ricketts felt that intellectual laziness and general mediocrity had infected the moral tone of the entire nation. It is so much easier emphatically to be right than to try to discover why you might be wrong.

> *December 31, 1900.* The mob is diseased by the mob, we are suffering from the effects of the majority Babel, and intellectual Hooliganism, a state of things so complicated and unimportant that old tests, based on a smaller and more intellectual experience, are no longer valid. Soon everything will be equally important, i.e. not important at all. This is the curse of the moment, and the curse of the many. The deeper-lying evil is the faculty not to act up to conviction, which characterizes the Britisher. He will know that a thing is right, but choose the easier course, because it is more convenient, or even without reason, by a perversion of instinct.

When confronted with physical expressions of what he considered this 'intellectual Hooliganism', it puts him into a 'cold self-possessed stupor'. His reaction to the news that the Velasquez Rokeby Venus had been damaged by a suffragette shows his strong feeling that art has no place in a political tug-of-war.

> *March 10, 1914.* I have been astonished at my unfeeling reception of the news: a cold self-possessed stupor at the imbecility of the act, a dim stupid wish for retribution – which is idiotic. I feel the time when the National Gallery and Museums will be held as hostages by revolutionaries, etc., is growing nearer.

The coming of the First World War temporarily diverted the attention of the nation from suffragettes, strikes and socialism. Ricketts's reaction to the war which was to become such a holocaust is similar to many who could not believe the terrors of modern warfare, yet he had an artist's sensitivity to the changes the war might bring to his life.

> *August 11, 1914.* The war has had one singular effect on my temper and character. I find myself more keenly interested in the beauty of things and in daily circumstances of life. I understand the invalid's interest in the details of mere existence, the relish of the convalescent for food, flowers, aspects of Nature, and a thousand things missed in the stress of daily life. Possibly I am over-hopeful, and in a sense optimistic, and feel that this terrible thing which is war will prove less terrible after all – that is less terrible than one had imagined. I hope I am not wrong in this, as I have so far been in everything else.

Though the war deeply affected Ricketts's consciousness of life and his attitude towards many of its aspects, its physical side was never a total reality. A few Zeppelin raids in Bloomsbury and Holborn could hardly compare with a soldier's life in the trenches.

> *Sept 11, 1915.* Decidedly there was something trivial and ignoble in this squalid wreckage and damage; city fires have left deeper traces on London streets. Nothing suggested the evidence of an act of war, but the stupid act of some scraggy anarchist with shot in a tin bomb, or the work of some hooligan rioters in a starving slum.

Knowledge of the high mortality rates, wretched trench conditions, and the ineptitude of the generals eventually permeated the consciousness of the men and women who kept the home fires burning. When the Armistice was announced, Ricketts records himself 'crying like a pig'. After the war, Ricketts's entries in his diary are less frequent and less analytical than before the war. Perhaps the changes in English intellectual and daily life were enough of a challenge in their own right to need no critique on their existence. He died of angina pectoris in 1931.

For another twentieth-century diarist the post-war years provided the perfect setting for his daily reminiscences. This was James Agate, whose nine volumes of *Ego* revealed to the English public the comfortable world of the successful drama critic. Agate was inspired to diary writing by the publication of Arnold Bennett's journal, and unlike some diarists, it seems clear that he intended his diaries to be published when he was alive as an extension of his other literary works. His first entry in the diary is a rationale of its existence.

June 3, 1932. Why am I keeping this diary? Answer. Because it is part of the insane desire to perpetuate oneself. Because there seem to be lots of things I want to say that other writers put into novels and accepted essayists into essays. Because it will be a relief to set down just what I do actually think, and in the first words to hand, instead of pondering what I ought to think and worrying about the words in which to express the hammered-out thought. But I cannot and never could invent a story, or be bothered to tell it, and have already published *five* books of essays, not having to do with the theatre, that have been complete and utter failures. So I am driven to this last ditch of expression.

James Agate was born in Pendleton, a part of Salford which he liked to think of as part of Manchester, in 1877. His father was a cotton manufacturer's agent. Agate saw a great deal of theatre as a child, but after a stint at Manchester Grammar School, he followed in his father's footsteps. Discontented with the cotton trade, he secured a post on the *Daily Dispatch*, though the lowness of the wages drove him to the *Manchester Guardian* where he worked under the distinguished critic C. E. Montague.

During the First World War, he was in France requisitioning hay, an eminently suitable task for a man with his passion for ponies.[1] After the war, he tried to set up a small

---

[1] 'Ego', Agate's title, was taken from the name of his favourite pony.

general store. It was a total failure. Still ambitious to write on the theatre, he had a lucky break in being appointed the dramatic critic for *The Saturday Review*. His first article appeared when he was forty-four. On 23 June 1923, he graduated to drama critic of the *Sunday Times*, and his reputation was made. He became the B.B.C.'s drama critic too, and edited collections of criticism. His spare time was spent with his beloved ponies, a hobby expensive enough to bring the bailiff to the door on occasion. He died in 1947.

Agate's diary often reads like a Maugham or Priestley play – a mirror of the languid 'thirties for those fortunate enough to have the money to languish. Sharing gossip and pleasantries, Agate records a pleasant world where boredom was the only danger. Actually he personally was in a precarious position. Continually living beyond his means, he was often told by his accountant that retrenchment was essential, but he could never quite justify economy to himself.

July 4, 1932. . . . Letter from Saunders, my charming accountant, saying that after allowing for rent, insurance, wages, income tax, instalments on car, cost of getting about, household expenses and re-imbursements, I cannot for the next twelve months reckon on more than a few shillings a day for myself. . . . For most people that ought to mean a competence. But I need a measure of luxury. I am thinking all the time about my work and cannot interrupt that thinking to climb on 'buses and find cheap restaurants. Also I write better when I have what I want.

When Agate did practise economy, it was more of the penny-wise pound-foolish variety. In an attempt to cut expenses he left one of his London flats and took up residence in Livingstone Cottage on Hadley Common. Of course he saved no money, but he was delighted with other aspects of his new home.

Nov. 12, 1933. . . . I have proved to myself *on paper*

that 3 houses with only 1 tenanted are as cheap as 2 houses fully inhabited. Also I hope to let the other two places at some price or other. Anyhow the decorations are charming, and judging by an address-book left behind, the previous tenants knew nobody less than an Earl. The basement is pitch-dark, and Wright, the chauffeur, thinks Livingstone, who lived here in 1857, camped in it as training for his life in darkest Africa.

Agate's patrician ambitions were shown in other ways besides interest in coroneted address books. After years of play-reviewing he contrasted the tedium of the modern play with the eternal freshness of his overriding passion, his ponies.

Sept 15, 1933. Plays and ponies. The waning interest is, I suppose, balanced by the increasing passion. I have got to the stage when all plays are alike in this, they are all too long and they all send me to asleep. I have lost delight in what might be called the common form of the theatre. I mean by this that I should like managers to pick out of each play that bit in which it differs from all the other plays, and then get me to the theatre to see it acted. This would take about twenty minutes. But the ponies are different. My age does not wither their infinite variety.

Agate's diaries are indeed a self-conscious extension of his personality and his need to see himself as a self-possessed gentleman rather than the ambitious Salford boy who made good. What keeps the diaries from becoming purely a testament to the mid-'thirties ethos of blasé urbanity is Agate's tremendous humour, and his ability to communicate his personal difficulties without whining about them. Nonetheless, it was a closed, exclusive and elite society that Agate, like so many of his diarist predecessors, wished to become part of, preferably without the strain of financial worries.

Society as seen by the admiring eye of Agate contrasts powerfully with the version of Evelyn Waugh. Waugh kept a diary pretty faithfully from the age of twelve (i.e. 1915) until a year before his death in 1966. When he died the manuscript diaries were lodged with an American university by his widow. They are believed to run to some quarter of a million words.

Apart from Virginia Woolf, Evelyn Waugh is the only English novelist of stature to be known to have kept a diary of what are more or less our own times. When Waugh died, the American news magazine *Time* described him as 'a flabby old blimp with brandy jowls and a menacing pewter complexion'. Another obituary emphasized his adoration of blue-blooded aristocracy and his contempt for the cult of the common man. Despite the generally acknowledged snobbery of the man for whom politics had been sliding headlong down a slippery slope since the Reform Bill of 1832, all the obituary-writers were justly concerned to recognize the extraordinary merits of his work. Waugh (whom Graham Greene described as 'the greatest novelist of my generation'), in book after book, and with finely chiselled prose, gave expression to a new and influential humour which was both sharp and imaginative. George Orwell, in a draft for a projected article on Waugh in 1949, noted 'W's driving forces. Snobbery, Catholicism', yet the end of his cryptic notes show how highly he regarded the novelist if not the man:

> Conclude. Waugh is abt as good a novelist as one can be (i.e. as novelists go today) while holding untenable opinions.

The importance of the Waugh diaries as a living record of some of the situations and characters that were transformed into the novels is considerable. He himself wrote:

> The novelist does not come to his desk devoid of experience and memory. His raw material is compounded of all he has seen and done . . .

One can confidently expect the next few decades to find many a post-graduate student quarrying the Waugh diaries in the University of Texas library to find the real-life equivalents of Brigadier Ritchie-Hook, or Apthorpe and his thunder-box, or Seth the Emperor or Sonia Digby-Van-Trumpington. And if the newspaper extracts are anything to go by, they should not have too much difficulty in so doing. However, raw material which has been prepared for us by the writer may well be found indigestible when served up uncooked. The inescapable conclusion to be formed from the diaries is that they can do little else but damage Waugh's reputation, and confirm the worst of the prejudices outlined in his obituaries. The man who emerges from their pages is a deeply unhappy man with a compulsion to view his fellow man through belladonna-tinted spectacles. With prose as baleful as his famous eye-bulging stare, he vents his spleen on friend and foe alike, as if determined to demonstrate that whatever cardinal virtues compose the Christian canon, four of them – prudence and temperance of the natural ones and hope and charity of the theological ones – held no particular attraction for him. Waugh describes his fellow Catholic and fellow novelist Graham Greene as 'always judging people by kindness'; it was not a quality Waugh himself could have been accused of having.

At the age of twelve he wrote of the vileness of the lower classes, and as he progressed in life, the targets became more specific – Noël Coward had no brains, Ramsay MacDonald was nasty and inadequate, Edmund Wilson an insignificant Yank, and the 1945–51 Labour governments composed of grey lice. Mixed up with the succession of cruel and gratuitous insults, many of them with seemingly no basis at all, are painful details of some of the dark nights of the soul that Waugh suffered. There are years when he hardly seems to have been sober from one month's end to another, drinking heavily to find an escape in oblivion. And yet when he records them in his diary in detail –

'unconsciousness punctuated with severe but well-directed vomitings' and the like – the reader gets the uncomfortable feeling that Waugh is boasting about them.

I suspect that the key to Waugh's nature was his deep desire to be loved, a desire given even more frenetic an impulse by his first wife's leaving him for another man. That desire can give some men the compulsion to be hail-fellow-well-met with the world and a craving for a host of admirers and flatterers, won by a capacity to amuse. A razor-sharp intellect and a nose for hypocrisy of the kind possessed by Evelyn Waugh meant that he could see such a sham for what it was. He adopted a different solution. By being as intolerable, insulting and unpleasant as he could, the fawning spaniels around his ankles waiting for crumbs from the famous novelist's table were driven yelping away. Only those who loved him enough to stay could be trusted (to a small circle of friends he was unswervingly loyal) and loved in return.

This is but a personal theory, but I can see no other explanation for an intelligent man like Waugh behaving so badly – tramping across Europe, a caricature of the Englishman abroad, dealing with uncomprehending Italians by adding the suffix 'o' to English words and shouting at them – unless it can be seen in broadly these terms. That he also became a Roman Catholic convert in 1930, the year after his first marriage failed, may also, perhaps, stem from his desire to accept the central tenet of Christian faith: that there is no body so vile or ill-behaved as ultimately to exclude itself from the all-embracing love of God.

BIBLIOGRAPHY

The Diary and Will of Elias Ashmole, edited and extended from the original manuscripts by R. T. Gunther (Oxford, 1927).
Diary of Mary Countess Cowper Lady to the Bedchamber to The Princess of Wales 1714–1720 (John Murray, 1864).

The Journal of Thomas Moore 1818–1841, edited by Peter Quennell (Batsford, 1964).

A Mid-Victorian Pepys, The Letters and Memoirs of Sir William Hardman, M.A., F.R.G.S., annotated and edited by S. M. Ellis (Cecil Palmer, London, 1923).

The Diary of Lady Frederick Cavendish, edited by John Bailey, vol. I (John Murray, 1927).

Self-Portrait Taken from the Letters & Journals of Charles Ricketts, R.A., collected and compiled by T. Sturge Moore, edited by Cecil Lewis (Peter Davies, 1939).

James Agate: *Ego* (Hamish Hamilton, 1938); *Ego 2* (Victor Gollancz, 1936); *Ego 3* (Harrap, 1938); *Ego 4* (Harrap, 1940); *Ego 5* (Harrap, 1942); *Ego 6* (Harrap, 1944); *Ego 7* (Harrap, 1945); *Ego 8* (Harrap, 1946); *Ego 9* (Harrap, 1948).

The Evelyn Waugh Diaries: extracts published in *The Observer Colour Magazine* from March to May 1973.

SEVEN

Far from the Madding Crowd

As a corrective to the magnification of trivial events within an enclosed and socially elevated circle of intimates, there is no better tonic than to read diaries kept by those who led their lives 'far from the madding crowd'. All the contrasts between town and country have been captured so beautifully by their respective diarists that to read one kind after the other is like taking a walk down a cool, leafy lane after a day spent in a hot and stuffy office. The most extraordinary thing of all is the way that one's priorities change in sympathy with the diarist's. In the company of Mary, Countess of Cowper, whether George I speaks to his son, the Prince of Wales, or not takes on a tremendous importance, and whether or not frost gets into the lettuce this year is a mere bagatelle. In the company of the Reverend James Woodforde, on the other hand, the fate of the lettuce is a burning question, and we could not care less whether the sovereign speaks or not.

If the Reverend James Woodforde had not kept a diary, we would not now know that he had ever drawn breath. In his time and since there have been thousands upon thousands of Woodfordes, about whom we know nothing at all, except in the most general sense – that they were clergymen who tended their local flock; that they married sons and daughters when necessary (and sometimes later); that they buried the dead; that they christened the newly living; and that they stood weekly in the pulpit to cast the dimmest of lights on biblical texts of their choice – excepting all that, we know nothing about them at all. And yet, in the case of James Woodforde, we know his daily routines

year in and year out almost as well as we know our own, for
in addition to catering for the religious welfare of his flock,
James Woodforde kept a diary.

Even that is something of an understatement, for the
Rev. Woodforde was a compulsive diarist *par excellence*. He
sat down to write his first entry in 1758 and he wrote on,
in a tiny, concentrated but clear hand, for the next forty-
five years, barely missing a day in all that time, and covering folio after folio of about seventy slim volumes by
1803. Unlike Thomas Moore, he never met famous men;
unlike Mary Cowper, events affecting the future of the
English throne were outside his ken; and unlike James
Boswell, he had no inner compulsion to know what made
him tick. That did not matter to him; he just scribbled on
regardless.

It has long been my conviction that Parkinson's famous
law – that work expands to fill the time available to do it
– needs a domestic and rural corollary. If, day after day,
there is nothing happening of major importance, then the
slightest thing which does happen must be made to seem
crucial. If, for example, one has nothing to do for the
next hour but make a cup of tea, then that act itself takes
on a whole new stature. The act which can be accomplished
in five minutes if there are more important things to be
done, swells now to a solemn and time-consuming ritual.
There is the kettle to be filled and placed on the flame.
There is the pot to be emptied, cleaned and warmed. There
is milk to be fetched, sugar to be measured, spoons to be
wiped, tea to be calculated. There is then the long wait
for the water to reach a precisely suitable temperature,
before the satisfying hiss as the hot water hits the dry and
thirsty tea leaves. And then, depending on your regional
preference, there is the standing, steeping, mashing or
stewing of the pot. Only after that can the pouring, the
stirring and the sipping start. Conversation and tea-drinking
being inseparable, the cup is quietly consumed to the sound
of good talk, preferably gossip rather than philosophic

discussion (for which wine or coffee are more suitable adjuncts), and when the pot has been finally emptied and the cups washed and dried, it will be found that the entire operation has lasted for some ninety minutes. And if this ritual act can be accomplished twice a day between the clearing of one meal and the preparations for the next, it can be made to fill an entire day.

It is this sort of daily routine which Woodforde invites us to share when we read him so that we readjust our own time scale from one where hour follows upon hour, to one where season follows upon season and year upon year with the same inevitability. Contrast for a moment the urgency with which James Boswell, the townsman, tries desperately to bed Louisa by the end of the week, with the patience of his contemporary James Woodforde, the country clergyman, looking for a wife. He is attracted by Miss Betsy White of Shepton Mallett on 25 September 1771:

> She is a sweet tempered girl indeed, and I like her much, and I think would make a good wife, I do not know but what I shall make a bold stroke that way ...

Bold strokes however take some thinking about and two years later, in August 1773, we hear that she has returned from London and that 'she is greatly improved and hand-somer than ever ...'. He still does not believe in rushing things, but on 28 May 1774 he takes a giant step;

> I went home with Betsy White and had some talk with her concerning my making her mine when an oppor-tunity offered and she was not averse to it at all.

The sweet-tempered Betsy, having reached this understand-ing, must have waited and waited for him, then decided she had waited too long. The entry for 10 August 1775 tells the whole story:

> Jenny Clarke returned from Devonshire last night. Betsy White of Shepton is to be married in a fortnight to a Gentleman of Devonshire by name Webster, a man

reported to have 500 Pd per annum, 10,000 Pd in the Stocks, besides expectations from his Father. He has settled 300 Pd per annum on Betsy.

Even the following month, he finds it difficult to forgive:

> Brother Heighes and myself took a walk in the evening down to Allhampton Field, and in our return back we met Mr. and Mrs. Webster in the Turnpike Road. Mrs. Webster spoke as usual to me, but I said little to her, being shy, as she has proved herself to be a mere Jilt . . .

Was it, one wonders, that £300 p.a. that tipped the balance, or was it the relief of finding a man who was prepared to propose and marry within a month?

The following year, Woodforde moved to Weston Longeville in Norfolk, a village with a population of perhaps 300, where he was joined by his niece Nancy,[1] and where the two of them settled down – he with someone to look after him, she with someone to look after – not so much to concentrate on living, as to start the long and patient wait for death. In this tiny, and extraordinarily ordinary, world, existence took on the ritual character mentioned earlier; meals become great signposts passed every few hours, taking on an ever-increasing importance as Parson Woodforde and his niece ate on regardless of the revolutions French and industrial:

> . . . for dinner a Couple of boiled Fowls and some Pork, a boiled plumb Pudding and a fine piece of rost Beef, roots etc . . .
> . . . a good dinner, surloin of Beef rosted, a Leg of Mutton boiled and plumb Puddings in plenty . . .
> I had a very fine Turkey for dinner to-day, and the best I ever tasted in my life . . .
> I gave them for dinner a couple of Rabbits smothered with onions, a Neck of Mutton boiled and a Goose rosted with a Currant Pudding and a plain one . . .

[1] For Nancy's views on these events, see pp. 190–3.

We had for dinner at Mr. Baldwin's, some fricasseed Rabit, some Mutton Stakes, a Piece of rost Beef, a fine plumb Pudding, Tarts and Syllabubs ...
We had for dinner a dish of Fish, some boiled fowls, some Bacon, a Tongue boiled, a Leg of Mutton rosted, some Oysters, Mince Pyes and Syllabubs. We had for supper fryed Herrings, Mutton, cold Tongue, Mince Pies, and Syllabubs and stewed Pears ...

In this orderly and well-fed world, anything beyond the norm becomes worth recording, perhaps the weather:

Never known scarce such fine weather at this season of the year, ... Thanks to God for such glorious weather ...
It rained very heavy in the Night a Thunder storm, with little Thunder or Lightning, but much Rain. All Nature seemed this morning greatly refreshed by the Rain, as it was so much wanted. Thanks be to the Lord for so blessed and gracious a Rain ...
Never known scarce such a continuation of so fine, mild and open Weather as we enjoy at this season ...

or something he had seen beyond his normal ken:

Mr. and Mrs. Custance are very agreeable people indeed, and both behaved exceedingly polite and civil to me [the Custances were the local gentry]. I there saw an Instrument which Mrs. Custance played on that I never saw or heard of before. It is called Sticcardo pastorale. It is very soft Music indeed. It is several long pieces of glass laid in order in a case, resting on each end of every piece of glass, and is played in the middle parts of the glasses by two little sticks with Nobbs at the end of them stricking the glass. It is a very small Instrument and looks when covered like a working Box for Ladies. I also saw the prettiest working Box with all sorts of things in it for the Ladies to carry with them when they go abroad, about as big again as a Tea Chest, that ever

I saw in my Life. It could not cost less than five guineas . . .

The sight of such wonders had him laying down his knife and fork and picking up his pen:

> Mr. Priest, a Mr. Ferman and myself went to see a remarkable large Pigg, which even exceeded our Idea of him. He is said to weigh 50 stone, is 9 foot from the Tip of his Tail to the Top of his Snout in length, and 4 foot high when standing. He is obliged to be helped up when down. I never saw such a Creature in my Life . . .

Messrs Priest and Herman may have seen a 'Pigg', but the Reverend Woodforde more probably saw a year's supply of bacon.

If we leave Woodforde for the moment and travel on a hundred years to mid-Victorian times, crossing the country, we find ourselves in the world of another diarist, the Reverend Francis Kilvert. Kilvert could not match Woodforde in years (he lived to be thirty-nine) or pages, though he kept his diary from 1870 until March 1879, and contrived to fill twenty-two notebooks with close script. He left a unique picture of country life, as seen by a curate and later vicar, of the border country where Breconshire, Radnorshire and Hereford all meet. For the duration of the diary, he was a bachelor, and although he met and married in August 1879, he died suddenly of peritonitis a month later.

Born in 1840, Kilvert was twenty-nine when he started his diary. A casual glance over his pages would suggest that nothing has changed since Woodforde's day. As the seasons change, the villagers still get into minor scrapes, and Toby, the diarist's cat, sits on the hearthrug in front of the fire. If we were to walk into his living-room, we feel we would be given the same sort of welcome that he was afforded when he paid his own little visits:

Oh the dear old Mill kitchen, the low, large room so snug, so irregular and full of old holes and corners, so cosy and comfy with its low ceiling, horse-hair couch, easy chair by the fire, flowers in the window recess, the door opening into the best room or parlour. Oh these kindly hospitable houses about these hospitable hills. I believe I might wander about these hills all my life and never want a kindly welcome, a meal, or a seat by the fireside.

His contentment with his lot is affecting. God is neither angry nor vengeful, but an avuncular figure settling comfortably into His favourite horse-hair armchair, as securely and certainly placed in Heaven as Queen Victoria or good King George were upon the throne: divinity and monarch in a benign partnership overseeing their subjects' spiritual and physical well-being. Above all, perhaps the most enviable aspect of Kilvert's life in Victorian England is his undying certainty that whatever the papers said of world affairs ('Reading the Mordaunt Warwickshire Scandal Case – Horrible disclosures of the depravity of the best London society'[1]), there was no doubt that the universe was unfolding generally in the way that it should.

Certainly, the weather could be severe. Both eighteenth and nineteenth centuries, so far as one can judge, had more extreme weather than the present one:

Preached at Clyro in the morning (Matthew xiv, 30). Very few people in Church, the weather fearful, violent deadly E. wind and the hardest frost we have had yet ... when I got to the Chapel my beard moustaches and whiskers were so stiff with ice that I could hardly open my mouth and my beard was frozen on to my mackintosh. There was a large christening party from Llwyn Gwilym. The baby was baptized in ice which was broken and swimming about in the Font.

[1] This was the divorce case in which Edward, Prince of Wales, had to appear as a witness.

. . . Pigs, sheep, calves swept away from meadow and cot and carried down the river with hundreds of tons of hay, timber, hurdles and, it is said, furniture. The roads swept bare to the very rock. Culverts choked and blown up, turnips washed out of the ground on the hillsides, down into the orchards and turnpike roads. Four inches of mud in the Rhydspence Inn on the Welsh side of the border the Sun, Lower Cabalva House flooded again and the carpets out to dry. Pastures covered with grit and gravel and rendered useless and dangerous for cattle till after the next heavy rain.

. . . The ground very slippery and dangerous, people walking along the ditches and going on all fours up Bredwardine Hill and across to the Lion Square. Emma Jones' mother came all the way from Dorstone to Bredwardine in the ditches. Price was obliged to go up the hill from the Cottage to his house on all fours and Janes Davies of Fine Street confessed to Dora that she had to crawl on the ice across the Lion Square on her hands and knees . . .

However, despite snow, flood and ice, Kilvert has the countryman's certitude that come Septuagesima he would be writing: 'The first snowdrops appeared in the Churchyard.'

For all the similarities, the passing of a century *has* seen some changes, if only in education: Kilvert is a more literate man than Woodforde, with a more acute eye for the world around him, and greater tolerance. Also, he has a sense of humour. If he remarks an example of country wit or wisdom, he records it for posterity:

Speaking of the necessity of renting land according to his capital the old farmer said, 'I couldn't cut rumps of beef out of mouse's legs.'

And if the local newspaper compositors are not up to scratch, he mentions that too:

The *Hereford Times* has misprinted our report of the Clytho Harvest Festival as follows. 'The *widows* are decorated with Latin and St. Andrew's crosses and other beautiful devices in moss with dazzling flowers'. This was irresistible.

Kilvert has a pleasing store of anecdotes too. In 1870, we read, a curate who took a candidate along for confirmation by an irate and impatient bishop was imperiously confirmed along with his candidate 'and the whole church was in a titter'. In 1871, on a trip to London, he himself was involved in a small but amusing incident. He visited a Burlington Arcade bookshop to enquire after a reproduction of a painting called 'Rock of Ages' only to have the shop owner back away and refuse to deal with him. It emerged later that the man was notorious for selling obscene photographs and had mistaken the reverend gentleman for a police spy.

He would have been disappointed if his own attitudes had been called parochial:

> Reading Edmund Jone's curious book ... an account of Aberystruth Parish, Monmouthshire. A ludicrous naive simplicity about his reflections and conclusions. He thinks Providence took particular pains in making his parish which he thinks one of the most wonderful in the world ...

The Reverend Woodforde could never have written that passage.

Kilvert's experience of musical novelty was, on the other hand, less fortunate than Woodforde's 'very soft Music indeed'. It also shows his delightful lack of pomposity:

> The schoolmaster is learning to play the violin. He produced the instrument and began to play upon it. It had a broken string, and there was something wrong with all the rest, and the noise it made 'fairly raked my bowels' as old Cord used to say at Wadham of Headeach's

violoncello. The schoolmaster however did not appear
to notice that anything was wrong. His wife held
the book up before him. 'Glory be to Jesus', sang the
schoolmaster, loudly and cheerfully sawing away at the
cracked and broken strings, while the violin screeched
and shrieked and screamed and groaned and actually
seemed to writhe and struggle in his arms like a wild
animal in agony. There was something so utterly incon-
gruous in the words and the noise, the heart-rending
bowel-raking uproar and screams of the tormented violin,
that I smiled. I could not help it. Shriek, shriek, scream,
groan, yell, howled the violin, as if a spirit in torment
were writhing imprisoned within it, and still the schoolmaster sawed away vigorously and sung amid the wailing,
screeching uproar, 'Glory be to Jesus' in a loud and
cheerful voice. It was the most ludicrous thing. I never
was so hard put to it not to laugh aloud.

Perhaps the only serious ripple to cross the smooth millpond
of Kilvert's existence was his continued celibacy. In 1871,
he approached the father of one of the village girls hoping
to make her his wife, but after a suspense of ten days, her
father sent him a cordial but firm refusal. These were the
days before a certain Viennese psychiatrist by the name of
Freud published his findings on sexuality. They were also
the days when it was possible for middle-aged and elderly
gentlemen to fondle, caress and kiss little girls without any
unfortunate interpretations being placed on their actions.
No less than Lewis Carroll, Kilvert was inordinately fond
of little girls:

... [She] looked shyly up to thank me from under her
long silky lashes.
... lithe, lissome, high-spirited, romping girls with their
young supple limbs, their white round arms, white
shoulders and brows, their rosy flushed cheeks, their
dark and fair curls tangled, tossed and blown back by
the wind, their bright wild saucy eyes, their red sweet

full lips and white laughing teeth, their motions as quick, graceful and active as young antelopes or fauns . . .

. . . Shall I confess that I travelled ten miles today over the hills for a kiss, to kiss that child's sweet face. Ten miles for a kiss . . .

. . . Being tub night Polly with great celerity and satisfaction stripped herself naked to her drawers before me and was very anxious to take off her drawers before me, but her grandmother would not allow her. As it happened the drawers in question were so inadequately constructed that it made uncommonly little difference whether they were off or on, and there was a most interesting view from the rear . . .

His favourite of all was Gypsy Lizzie who had been placed in his reading class. He confided his daydreams of her to his diary:

The sun . . . has kissed the fair hand and arm that lies upon the coverlet and the white bosom that heave half uncovered after the restlessness of the sultry night, and has kissed her mouth whose scarlet lips, just parting in a smile and pouting like rosebuds to be kissed, show the pearly gleam of the white teeth, and has kissed the sweet face and the blue veined silky lashed eyelids and the white brow and the soft tangled hair, till she has unclosed the sweetest eyes that ever opened to the dawn, and risen and unfastened the casement and stood awhile breathing the fresh fragrant mountain air as it blows cool upon her flushed cheek and her half-veiled bosom, and lifts and ruffles her bright hair which still keeps the kiss of the sun . . .

Can we doubt that Kilvert would, in this case, like to have been the sun? As a diarist, he unconsciously tells us more than he would perhaps have wished, if not more than he ever knew.

Woodforde and Kilvert are self-revealing in ways which

would be far less likely among more sophisticated men, and certainly much of the pleasure in reading them stems from their naïvety. The trained and polished writer has to do by art what they do naturally – to address us unaffectedly and directly. When other considerations are allowed to take the upper hand, when the religious diarist, say, makes his youth seem blacker than it was in order to increase the drama of a later conversion to the straight and narrow, our enjoyment of the work is less.

Such thoughts are prompted by a twentieth-century diary kept by the distinguished author Henry Williamson. Specifically kept for a year with publication in mind, it reached the bookstalls in 1937 under the title *Goodbye West Country*. In it, the man with so intimate and touching a relationship with nature, demonstrated so conclusively in his classic *Tarka the Otter*, tells us of his flying, motoring, walking, angling, and bird-watching activities. *Tarka* was written when Williamson rejected the rest of mankind after the First World War and lived a hermit-like existence in North Devon. His views on urban man are made equally clear in this diary:

> Most men who work in cities strive, I suppose, for competence to escape the toil and nervous strains of mass-men. The by-products of that city-toiling, of those nervous strains are mental confusions, spurious humanitarianism, maladies of ill-adjustment, no roots in the soil . . .

He continues too to demonstrate his wonderful ability to describe natural phenomena and to conjure superb images to share with his readers: 'In summer the air over the fields of Sedgemoor crinkles and slurs the landscape with its stagnant heat . . .' When he catches a salmon and takes it home, we are forcefully hit by the true meaning of what has happened:

> I carried it home by my tattered red silk handkerchief

tied to tail and jaw – a curved ingot of silver. Soon the dreamy azure was gone, with the faint coral tinge of its fin, all the spirit of its ocean god vanished from it, as it lay on a dish in the larder, something to eat . . .

It seems a tragedy that some of the best writers on nature seem to need to compensate for their identification with wild life with an anti-humanist approach to man himself, as if the one identification excludes the other. Williamson would dismiss this as sentimental effete liberalism perhaps, but I think it is his inability to come to terms with the most diverse and complicated animal of all, man, that made him prone to fall hook, line and sinker for the totalitarian philosophies abroad in the 'thirties. In the diary he quotes a letter he received from a newspaper editor in defence of his thesis that he was being gagged politically. Says the editor: 'I am all with you when it comes to salmon and otter but violently opposed to your ideas of the great Mr. Hitler . . .'

There are so many good things in *Goodbye, West Country* that the interlude spent in Nazi Germany where he was an admiring observer ('The feeling I had while among the mass of people listening to Adolf Hitler at Nurnberg was one of their happiness and goodness') and his theories that the Fuehrer was merely misunderstood, and made to appear a monster, a madman and a degenerate by Jewish-owned and Jewish-edited newspapers, intrude so appallingly into the West Country world of the diary that one cannot fail to conclude that the editor was the perceptive one, and Williamson the man wearing blinkers. Kilvert in April 1870 had been horrified by the presence of two sightseers at the ruins of Llanthony Abbey:

> Of all noxious animals too the the most noxious is a tourist. And of all tourists the most vulgar, illbred, offensive and loathsome is the British tourist . . .

Political theory in the West Country is equally noxious, but the most vulgar, illbred, offensive and loathsome is Fascism.

BIBLIOGRAPHY

Reverend James Woodforde: *The Diary of a Country Parson*, edited by John Beresford in 5 volumes (Humphrey Milford, London, 1924–1931).

Kilvert's Diary, edited by William Plomer in 3 volumes (Cape, 1938–40). A one-volume selection, also edited by William Plomer, was published by Cape in 1944 and reprinted in 1961 and 1969.

Henry Williamson: *Goodbye, West Country* (Putnam, 1937).

EIGHT

Of Writers and Writing

Many writers who are able to deal with their own experiences in fictional form never choose, or perhaps are not able, to convey them directly in the form of autobiography or diary. Whatever the reasons, it is a fact that the number of writers who keep or have kept diaries are in a tiny minority, and those who keep 'literary' diaries even fewer in number. For present purposes at least, a 'literary' diary is one about writers and writing, one which provides insights either into the creative process or into working methods. The literary diary therefore need not necessarily tell us much about the more external aspects of a writer's life.

The journal of Mary Shelley, which was kept intermittently from 1814 to 1840, is a case in point. The diary is more likely to be consulted by the biographer for information on Shelley than on Mary. Some of the most important events in her own life are omitted or recorded in very cryptic fashion. On 24 July 1816 she starts work on the novel *Frankenstein*, one of the few minor novels of the time which is still read today, but her entry reads laconically: 'I read "Nouvelles Nouvelles" [by Madame de Genlis] and write my story.' Frequently, in subsequent months, even this is reduced to 'Write'. The writing of the diary is sometimes taken over by Shelley himself. On 22 February 1815 he tells us that she is 'in labour, and, after a few additional pains, she is delivered of a female child . . .'. Mary resumes the entries herself four days later, and on 6 March she records the subsequent event very cryptically: 'Find my baby dead. Send for Hogg. Talk. A miserable day. In the evening read "Fall of the Jesuits". Hogg sleeps here.' It is not that the death leaves her unaffected:

> *March 13th, 1815* Shelley and Clara go to town. Stay at home; net, and think of my little dead baby. This is foolish, I suppose; yet, whenever I am left alone to my own thoughts, and do not read to divert them, they always come back to the same point – that I was a mother and am one no longer . . .
>
> *March 19, 1815* Dream that my little baby come to life again; that it had only been cold, and that we rubbed it before the fire, and it lived. Awake and find no baby. I think about the little thing all day. Not in good spirits . . .

The terseness of the entries does not disguise the importance of the loss.

Mary was born Mary Godwin on 30 August 1797. She was the daughter of William Godwin, the philosopher and political writer who was then deeply in debt and producing unreadable books, and of Mary Wollstonecraft, the author of *Vindication of the Rights of Woman*. They had married five months before to legitimize the birth of Mary. Tragedy was to be a companion of Mary's from the first few hours of her life, for in giving birth to her, her mother died. She grew up blaming herself for her mother's death, and spent hours reading at her mother's tomb in the St Pancras cemetery. Perhaps literature was her sole escape, for at home her father's second marriage, to Mrs Clairmont, brought her a step-mother who hated her and a hysterical step-sister (who joined a melancholic half-sister, the daughter of her mother by a previous liaison, who was later to commit suicide).

Mary could have been forgiven for seizing on any opportunity for escape, even if it had been to the dullest of conventional marriages. But being her parents' daughter, she was more likely to be won by intellect than income. Before her seventeenth birthday, she had fallen desperately in love with Percy Bysshe Shelley and eloped with him.

This was not a simple matter. Shelley, though only twenty-one himself, was an unhappy husband and father already, having run away with and married Harriet Westbrook two years before. (The marriage had already been wrecked by Harriet and her sister Eliza, though Harriet was pregnant again.) On this second elopement, Shelley took Claire, Mary's step-sister, with them.

Mary and Shelley were not able to marry until the end of 1816, a few weeks after Harriet had drowned herself in the Thames, pregnant by another man, and only a few months after the suicide by poison of Mary's half-sister.

This is the background against which we read Mary's diary, which provides a remarkably comprehensive picture of the books she and Shelley read as they wandered around Europe, pursued by his creditors. Having hitched her wagon to a comet, she consumed literature at the same fiery pace as he did:

Mar 11 [*1820*] Finish the 'Age of Reason' [Thomas Paine]. Ride out with Mr. Mason. Shelley reads the 'Fall of Sejanus' [Ben Jonson] aloud, and 'Hobbes on Man'.
Mar 12 Read 'Rights of Man' [Thomas Paine]; write, ride.
Mar 13 Read 'Rights of Man'; ride. Shelley reads Hobbes, and 'Catiline's Plot' aloud.
Mar 14 Move to other lodgings. Write. Read 'Rights of Man'.
Mar 15 Read 'Rights of Man'. Call at Casa Silva. Shelley reads Hobbes; finishes 'Catiline's Plot'.
Mar 16 Read 'Rights of Man'. Shelley reads Hobbes . . .

And so the pair read on, eagerly extending their knowledge of politics, history and literature, and occasionally stopping to translate Spinoza together.

So long as she was with Shelley, Mary was absorbed by him and her love for him, though it is not true that she was completely under his shadow. Her famous novel *Franken-stein* stemmed from a conversation between Shelley and

Byron on galvanism and corpses, but for a nineteen-year-old girl it was remarkably original. It is impossible to know what she might have later achieved, but for one thing: on 8 July 1822 Shelley, her genius, lover and husband, was drowned.

In one sense, Mary's life was over, though it had another thirty years to run. The diary breaks off abruptly on 7 July, the day before the drowning, and it does not resume until October. In place of the terseness of the past, she now confides not so much events as her impassioned feelings for the life she has lost.

> For eight years I communicated, with unlimited freedom, with one whose genius, far transcending mine, awakened and guided my thoughts. I conversed with him; rectified my errors of judgment; obtained new lights from him; and my mind was satisfied. Now I am alone – oh, how alone! The stars may behold my tears, and the wind drink my sighs; but my thoughts are a sealed treasure, which I can confide to none . . . now, I am reduced to those white pages, which I am to plot with dark imagery . . .

The rest of the journal, like her life, was mainly devoted to Shelley. She brought up her son, who was eventually to inherit his father's baronetcy, turned down three proposals of marriage (including one from Washington Irving), brought out an edition of Shelley's literary remains, and started a biography of Shelley which was destined never to be finished. Although she lived until 1851, perhaps she wrote her own finest epitaph when she recorded in her diary in October 1838: 'Books do much; but the living intercourse is the vital heat. Debarred from that, how have I pined and died!'

On 20 November 1825, three years after Shelley had died, and while Mary mourned, a highly successful novelist began to keep a diary for the first time in his life. He was fifty-four. A little less than seven years later, he was dead, but the journal he kept during those last years has been rightly acclaimed as a classic of the diary form. The diarist was Sir Walter Scott, and the years were perhaps the unhappiest of his life.

In 1825 he published *The Betrothed* and *The Talisman*, the latter one of the most popular of the Waverley novels. Since his early days, he had changed his ideas on Napoleon radically and he now embarked on the extensive research necessary for a massive nine-volume biography. In July he had been to Ireland with his daughter Annie and his biographer Lockhart, where he had been lionized even in the streets of Dublin, where 'the mob and boys huzza'd as at the chariot wheels of a conqueror'.

Scott could write with great rapidity; he had been enjoying success as a famous writer since 1807, but despite this rosy picture of a successful writer continuing on his prolific and heralded way, all was not well. When he began his journal, concern was already being expressed that the publishing and printing firms with which he was financially involved might run into difficulty. In fact, 1825 had been a year of feverish financial speculation in London and the bill-backed credit that sustained the firms was beginning to crumble.

Scott had bought two small vellum-bound volumes with built-in locks, in which he started light-heartedly to jot down the incidents of the day, but after only two days there was a very distinct change in tone:

Here is a matter for a May morning, but much fitter for a November one. The general distress in the city has affected H. and R. [Hurst, Robinson & Co.], Constable's great agents [Archibald Constable, the publisher]. Should they GO it is not likely that Constable can stand, and such an event would lead to great distress and per-plexity on the part of John Ballantyne and myself. Thank God I have enough at least to pay fifty shillings in the pound, taking matters at the very worst.

The morrow brings no better news:

> Constable has been here as lame as a duck upon his legs, but his heart and courage as firm as a rock. He has convinced me that we will do well to support the London House. He has sent them £5,000 and proposes we should borrow on our joint security £5,000 for their accommodation. J. B. and R. Cadell [another publisher] present. I must be guided by them and hope for the best. Certainly to part company would be to incur an awful risk.

On the 25th, Sir Walter was making resolutions:

> No more building
> No more purchases of land till times are quite safe
> No buying books or expensive trifles

He was glad to leave such thoughts behind him when he went out for a walk:

> No man that ever stopped on heather has less dread than I of catching cold; and I seem to regain, in buffeting with the wind, a little of the high spirit with which in younger days I used to enjoy a Tam O'Shanter ride through darkness, wind and rain . . .

Regrettably, it was a dreadful financial cold he was about to catch. On 17 January James Ballantyne and Co. stopped payments after Constable had done the same, having failed to raise more credit. Scott was ruined.

> *January 22, 1826* . . . I feel neither dishonoured nor broken down by the bad – miserably bad – news I have received. I have walked my last on the domains I have planted – safe the last time in the halls I have built. But death would have taken them from me if misfortune is just another dye to turn up against me in this run of ill-luck i.e. if I should break my magic wand in the fall from this elephant, and lose my popularity with my fortune. Then *Woodstock* [the novel he was currently working on]

and *Boney* may both go to the papermaker, and I may take to smoking cigars and drinking grog, and turn devotee, and intoxicate the brain another way. In prospect of absolute ruin ... I find my eye moistening, and that will not do. I will not yield without a fight ...

Just how bonny a fighter Sir Walter was is amply shown by his remaining years. Even when his friends offered money to settle his debts he is reported to have said 'No! This right hand shall work it all off!' As a result of the defaults, he was landed with debts of over £116,000. Now he was working not for himself but for his creditors. His health was in decline – rheumatism, chilblains and a worsening of the lameness which he had had since contracting infantile paralysis as a child. But there was no bitterness, even when he had to leave the home where he had spent the last twenty-five years: 'So farewell ... and may you never harbour worse people than those who now leave you ...' Instead he put his right hand to work. In 1827 he published *Chronicles of the Canongate* (including 'The Two Drovers'), as well as the massive work on Napoleon; and between 1828 and 1831, four series of tales on Scottish history and four novels, including *The Fair Maid of Perth*, plus a variety of other smaller works. And at the same time he kept up his journal, despite having had ample justification to throw down his pen in disgust after filling his daily quota of words. If it can be said that some of the works were below his best, it can also be said that he had every excuse. In February 1830 he had the first of a series of strokes that cost him a paralysis and loss of speech. His doctor ordered him to rest; instead, he plunged himself into annotating a collected edition of the Waverley novels.

Although he was the highest of high Tories, the Whig government showed enough compassion to put a ship at his disposal that he might have a cruise in the winter of 1831–2. He shows in his journal that he had periods of mental confusion. There were more strokes and in April 1832 he had finally to abandon his journal. He died in September at home in Scotland leaving, in addition to his novels, in themselves a lasting contribution to English literature, a journal which for its portrayal of fortitude in adversity and stoical resignation to the malignities of fate will remain a classic example of the diarist's art.

Scott's diary might be chosen as a superb demonstration of what a diary can become when the man writing it is an artist with an artist's capacity for objectivity. The diary of Henry Crabb Robinson, on the other hand, reveals a man with an infinite love for literature, with personal charm, with an unparalleled circle of literary acquaintances, with the patience and dedication to sustain him through thirty-five closely-written diaries, thirty volumes of journals, thirty-two volumes of letters, four volumes of reminiscences, and one volume of anecdotes; yet without the ability to reproduce in his diary even a fraction of the interest of his long life.

Crabb Robinson was born in Bury St Edmunds in 1775, the youngest son of a tanner. He received a no-more-than-adequate education at a selection of small private schools and was articled to a solicitor in 1790. One might conclude that his fate had already been decided. He would make a safe but dull marriage, potter around the law courts, and retire at the usual age to cultivate his garden. In the next eight years, he heard John Wesley preach, and Henry Erskine conduct a case, but they were his only claims to anything out of the ordinary. Then, in 1798, he was left a legacy by an uncle which guaranteed him £100 *per annum* henceforth.

He must have had hidden depths for he took this as a basis for changing his life totally. He took off for the Continent, and finished up in Germany, where not only did he meet Goethe and Schiller, but enrolled himself at Jena University to study. Leaving there in 1802, he travelled on, met Madame de Staël in France, and in 1805 left for home on the same boat that brought news of the Battle of

Austerlitz. Back in this country, he went straight to Charles James Fox (Foreign Secretary at this time) and asked for a job befitting his new stature as linguist and European traveller. He did not get it, but he did manage to become a correspondent for *The Times*, and in no time at all he was made Foreign Editor. He sent back despatches from Corunna and from the Peninsular War, but had not yet totally forsaken the law, for in 1813 we find him called to the Bar. His own intent was to quit the Bar only when he was earning £500 a year. This he did in 1828 and he kept his word, adding that the two wisest acts of his life were joining the Bar and leaving it.

By now, he could add to his contacts with the German masters close friendships with Lamb, Coleridge, Wordsworth and Southey. When Wordsworth went off on an Italian tour in 1837 it was Robinson that he chose as a companion, and Robinson to whom he dedicated his account of the tour. Somehow Robinson also found time to become prominent in the anti-slavery campaign, to be elected a Fellow of the Society of Arts, and to be a founder of both the Athenaeum and University College, London. He died at his home in Russell Square at the age of ninety-one.

Among the people he had met were Landor, Carlyle, Disraeli, Macready, Hazlitt and de Quincey, and yet Crabb Robinson could make them all sound as dull as his next-door neighbours. There are hundreds of details which are not with*out* interest, but there is no spark, no real life, in the entries. If only he had had the literary ability of even one of his friends, what an unforgettable journal he might have produced.

March 3rd, 1832 ... We were joined by John [Stuart] Mill, certainly a young man of great talent. He is deeply read in French politics, and spoke judiciously enough about them, bating his, to me, unmeaning praise of Robespierre for his incomparable talents as a speaker –

being an irresistible orator – and the respect he avowed for the virtues of Mirabeau . . .

Crabb Robinson adds little or nothing to what we already know of J. S. Mill, and is equally unforthcoming when describing a visit, with some friends, to the Lambs:

> *September 28th, 1832* . . . We had scarcely an hour to chat with them; but it was enough to make both Landor and Worsley express themselves delighted with the person of Mary Lamb; and pleased with the conversation of Charles Lamb, though I thought him by no means at his ease, and Miss Lamb was quite silent. Nothing in the conversation recollectable . . .

This is at least part of the trouble; where a great diarist like Boswell can go home and recreate the spirit if not the letter of what was said, Crabb Robinson cannot:

> *January 13, 1836* . . . Wordsworth's conversation has been very interesting lately, and had I not so bad a memory, that a few hours suffice to obscure all I have heard, I might insert many a remarkable opinion if not fact . . .

He once excused himself to Wordsworth for writing so seldom because he rarely had anything to say he thought Wordsworth would find worth reading. It is the attitude of a loyal and sincere friend but not, alas, a 'good' diarist.

The same criticism might be levelled against the novelist George Gissing. Though the contents of his journal afford little information about the main events of his life, the extracts published in *Letters of George Gissing to Members of his Family* provide an invaluable guide to the novelist, though perhaps less to the man. He himself believed the keeping of a diary to be important, and not only to writers. In a letter to his sister in June 1880 he wrote:

> By the by, do you keep a diary? If not, I should certainly advise you to do so, now that you have more time to

spare. Put in it all the main events of each day, and, at the same time, every book you read, with remarks upon them. Likewise jot down special thoughts that come into your head. To say nothing of the pleasure it gives you to look over such a book in future days, you benefit much by the careful thought it necessitates, thoughts about yourself as well as other things and other people . . .

Although the advice was good, he by no means followed it himself. The diary did have an attraction for him. however. He began his first in 1870 at the tender age of thirteen. It lasted only a week, but is a happy blend of the public and private:

> This morning no fresh War news [i.e. the Franco-Prussian War]. Germans still marching on Paris. According to expectations Algie began his turn of mumps this morning, which I have happily got over . . .

He included anything which took his fancy, on one occasion adding the firm, if pompous, justification: 'because I think it a fact worthy of attention.' He duly recorded the following information:

> The number of eggs deposited by certain of the oviparous species of fish is enormous. The sole lays 100,000. The carp 200,000. The tench 400,000. The mackerel 500,000. The flounder 1,300,000. The cod 8,500,000. The salmon 20,000,000.

Gissing was born in 1857, the son of a Wakefield chemist. Judging by the interest and enthusiasm for knowledge he displays in this early short-lived diary, he was a brilliant pupil. At fifteen he won a scholarship to Owens College, Manchester, which prepared students for the intermediate examinations of the universities of Oxford, Cambridge and London. (The college later became Manchester University.) Here his brilliant progress continued. He won various honours and prizes, and it was assumed by everyone that he would go on to university and become an academic. Instead, he fell madly in love with a young prostitute, and to save her from the streets, began to steal from his fellow students. A strictly amateur thief, he was soon caught, expelled, sent briefly to prison, then packed off to America.

Still only nineteen, he scratched the barest of livings there by teaching and writing. This lasted for a year until he returned to England, tracked down the prostitute and married her. They had nothing in common at all, but he supported them by giving private lessons until she, by then a dipsomaniac, left him to return to her old trade. Somehow, on the verge of starvation, he scraped a living as a hack writer, an experience which led to the publication of *New Grub Street* in 1891. If he kept a journal during this period, it has not been preserved.

He started again, apparently, at the end of December 1887. His preoccupation with his writing is self-evident:

> *January 25th, 1888* A terrible day, got up with a headache, from 9.30 to 2 wrote – or rather struggled to write – achieving not quite two pages. Suffered anguish worse than any I can remember in the effort to compose . . . At 7 tried to write again, and by 9.0 finished one page . . .

He was always prone to depression (his brother wrote that he was more likely to be adversely affected by the weather than anyone he had ever met), and there were many days when writing was difficult:

> *May 8th, 1888* A day of blankest idleness and misery. Afternoon to Grosvenor where I got Volume 1 of Hardy's *Wessex Tales* and Volume II of Vernon Lee's *Journalia*. Read them both in an hour and a half then paced my rooms in an agony of loneliness, this becomes intolerable; in absolute truth I am now and then on the verge of madness. This life I *cannot* live much longer, it is hideous.
>
> *May 20th, 1888* This morning beheld an idiotic experi-

ment. I rose at 5.30 (glorious sunshine), made a cup of cocoa at 6 o'clock, and sat down – to write! The result was that by 7 o'clock I had written five words, and had fretted myself into a headache. This has solved decisively the question of Walter Scottian work in my case. It is wholly out of the question.

He went to Italy at the end of the year, but in 1889 he returned to settle in Exeter where he was to remain for two years. The change of locale did not help.

October 3rd, 1889 Have grown tired of noting the monotonous and ignoble days. My solitude is a wearisome topic.
October 7th, 1889 Did nothing. Thought nothing.

He had published his first novel, *Workers in the Dawn*, nine years earlier (he had been obliged to finance the printing himself after receiving a sheaf of rejection slips), but he produced novels throughout the 1880s and was establishing a solid reputation if an insufficient income. Whatever inner masochistic compulsion had lead him to marry Nell Harrison, the prostitute, now reasserted itself, and in 1891 he married a servant-girl he had picked up in Regent's Park. It was not a success ('*December 31st, 1892* The year 1892 on the whole profitless. Marked by domestic misery and discomfort . . .') and it was probably a relief when the girl, a vicious shrew, died mad.

By the turn of the century, his reputation had continued to grow and the hideous poverty of his early days was behind him. By rights, despite his intermittent lung trouble, he should have been able to enjoy a long and fruitful period of creativity and affluence.

April 7th, 1902 Yesterday chanced to open the first volume of my *Diary* and found it such strange and moving reading, that I have gone on, hour after hour. Who knows whether I may not still live a few years; and if so,

I shall be sorry not to have a continuous record of my life. So I resolve to begin journalising once more, after all but a year of intermission . . .

In fact he abandoned the diary at the end of 1902, and a year later he died of pneumonia at the age of forty-seven. H. G. Wells was at his death-bed (and drew upon the experience when describing the death of Uncle Ponderevo in *Tono-Bungay*), nursing him through to the end. Gissing's novels, with their uncompromising picture of life at the bottom of the scale, will live on. It would be a pity if his fragmentary diary, which demonstrates the agony of the writer struggling to work, were to be totally forgotten.

If Gissing's diary catalogues the multitude of difficulties to which a writer may succumb, then Arnold Bennett's, even more than Sir Walter Scott's, shows what it is to be able to write day in and day out to schedule, and to the achievement of fame and fortune. His was the right hand to put even Scott's to shame. To add to the enormous word-count of his novels, his reviews and his articles, must be added his journals which, kept from 1896 to 1929, account for no less than another million words.

Bennett was a great one for reassuring himself in his diaries that his creative powers were unimpaired. Not for him the agonies of a Gissing:

January 2nd, 1899 If I gained nothing else last year, I gained facility. In the writing of sensational fiction I made great strides during the last few months, and with ordinary luck I could now turn out a complete instalment (about 4,000 words) after 3 o'clock in an afternoon. For critical work too, I have become much faster and more adroit.

January 2nd, 1905 Last year I wrote 282,100 words, exclusive of re-writing. This comprises two plays with Eden Phillpotts, *Christina* and *An Angel Unawares*, the greater part of *A Great Man*, also a series of facetious short stories entitled 'The Adventures of Jack Stout' and one other short story. I don't think I ever did anything like so much creative work in one year . . .

December 31st, 1907 I spent just over 23,000 frs. this year, and earned about 32,000 frs. I wrote *The Statue* (with E.P.[1]), and *Sole Survivors* (with E.P.), *Love and Riches*, *Death of Simon Fuge*. Five other short stories. First part of *The Old Wives' Tale*. About 46 newspaper articles. And my journal. Also my play *Cupid and Commonsense*, and scenario of a new humorous novel, *The Case of Leek* [published as *Buried Alive*]. Grand total: 375,000 words. This constitutes a record year.

Like an athlete following a training schedule religiously, in hopes of winning a gold medal, from 1 January to 31 December, seven days a week, Arnold Bennett notched up his minimum wordage. The routine that for most writers is a necessary discipline was for him a fetish. Breakfast had to be on the table to the minute, and the house silent as the grave (even the dog had to be kept quiet) until the daily total had been exceeded. With what success this was achieved is evident in the entries above – if there had been an award for fecundity, Bennett would have won it.

Such a track record suggests that as a writer Bennett can have been little better than a paid hack. That is precisely how many have sought to describe him – with tinges of jealousy and fastidiousness in about equal proportions. But the skill displayed in his major novels is certain proof of his stature as a writer.

Bennett was born in 1867, the eldest son of a domineering Staffordshire solicitor who did his best to force his son into the legal profession. When Bennett first came to London, it was as a costing clerk to a firm of solicitors. He became a writer by accident. Persuaded by his landlord to enter a *Tit Bits* literary competition, he won first prize. After that, perhaps to escape the tyranny of his father, he

---

[1] Eden Phillpotts.

entered journalism and eventually became editor of a magazine, long since defunct, called *Woman*. He turned out well-
paid if worthless pulp fiction, but after some difficult
years, at the age of twenty-seven he produced his first
serious novel *A Man from the North*. It was recommended
to John Lane the publisher by no less a figure than John
Buchan, but it did not win Bennett instant fame and
fortune. There were more potboilers to follow, but it was
only through the help of a literary agent who believed in
him sufficiently to give him financial assistance that he was
able to go to Paris, where it was still possible to live
cheaply. He married a Frenchwoman who had been both his
secretary and his mistress, and although the marriage was a
failure, it brought him a temporary peace.

On 18 November 1903, he was in a French restaurant
when a fat and vulgarly dressed middle-aged woman began
changing tables as he ate:

> . . . And the whole restaurant secretly made a butt of
> her. She was repulsive; no one could like her or sym-
> pathize with her. But I thought – she has been young
> and slim once. And I immediately thought of a long 10
> or 15 thousand words short story, 'The History of Two
> Old Women'. I gave this woman a sister, fat as herself.
> And the first chapter would be in the restaurant (both
> sisters) something like tonight – and written rather
> cruelly. Then I would go back to the infancy of these
> two, and sketch it all. One should have lived ordinarily,
> married prosaically, and become a widow. The other
> should have become a whore and all that; 'guilty splen-
> dour'. Both are overtaken by fat. And they live together
> in old age, not too rich, a nuisance to themselves and to
> others. Neither has any imagination . . . The two lives
> would have to intertwine. I saw the whole work quite
> clearly, and hope to do it.

From that incident and that passage in his journal, and after
a few years of gestation, Bennett was to construct his

superb novel *The Old Wives' Tale*. Before he began it he told his agent that it would be a great novel – it was. It brought him fame and fortune (in the United States before Britain), and other novels, *The Card* and *Clayhanger* among them, followed thick and fast. He became a national figure and Lord Beaverbrook, who used him as a Director of Propaganda in the First World War, bought his services for the *Evening Standard* – at the rate of £300 a month for one weekly book page. The money continued to accumulate: he acquired a Rolls, a yacht and all the trappings of luxury. He turned out many novels below his best, yet, when his detractors began to murmur that he was a literary giant no longer capable of writing well, he produced *Riceyman Steps*, another masterpiece.

His *Journals* are interesting not only for the light they throw upon his work and life: they are the observations of a sensitive man recorded with candour but without malice – a testament to a born writer who could never bring himself to stop writing. In his journal, he wrote that the essential characteristic of a really great novelist was 'a Christ-like, all-embracing compassion'. In the sense that he had compassion and love for ordinary people and ordinary things, Bennett was at his best, a great novelist with a capacity to reach a very wide audience. However, neither his love for the ordinary nor his phenomenal social and financial success served to endear him to the woman novelist who was one of his sharpest critics.

This was Virginia Woolf, a diarist and major novelist whose concepts of life and literature could hardly be more at odds with Bennett's. Where Bennett, despite the handicap of a stammer which became almost a trademark, liked to move in the social circles to which his fame had brought him, she was shy, reserved and, frankly, a romantic snob. Where he could sit down with a pile of paper and produce page after page of prose like an automaton, she wrote and rewrote and polished and slaved over the first paragraph of the most unimportant of reviews. Where his name was

world-wide, her name was meaningless outside a small
côterie. She published few books compared with the vast
corpus of work put out by Bennett.

Her diary was kept from 1915 to 1941, up to four days
before her death. The twenty-seven manuscript volumes
of her diary, written on separate sheets which were later
bound up, were left by her late husband Leonard Woolf
to the Berg Collection of the New York Public Library,
and his selection, published in 1953 under the title *A
Writer's Diary*, suggests that Virginia Woolf is one of the
foremost diarists of the twentieth century. Leonard Woolf's
reasons for his selection of entries (mostly those relevant
to her writing in a narrow sense) were there set out:

> The diary is too personal to be published as a whole
> during the lifetime of many people referred to in it. It
> is, I think, nearly always a mistake to publish extracts
> from diaries and letters, particularly if the omissions
> have to be made in order to protect the feelings or reputa-
> tions of the living. The omissions almost always distort
> or conceal the true character of the diarist or letter-writer
> and produce spiritually what an Academy picture does
> materially, smoothing out the wrinkles, warts, frowns,
> and asperities.

In *A Writer's Diary*, his wife's portrait of Arnold Bennett
could not be said to have undergone much retouching.
She had long considered him, and his fellow Edwardian
novelists Galsworthy and Wells, out of date, materialistic,
and prone to mistake faithfulness of exterior detail for
inner truth. She said so in print on more than one occasion.
He did not reply. However, when her *Jacob's Room* was
published in the early 1920s, Bennett was given it to
review. Praising the work for its exquisite writing and for
its striking originality, he ventured the relatively mild
opinion that there was, none the less, something of a flaw
in the author's characterization.

This rankled a good deal with her. She wrote in her diary,

'People, like Arnold Bennett, say I can't create, or didn't in *Jacob's Room*, characters that survive . . .', and by the end of 1923 she had published the first version of her famous essay 'Mr. Bennett and Mrs. Brown', which was to be published and republished and given as a public lecture, reiterating her feelings on Bennett's inadequacies as a novelist.

If it appears that she was being morbidly self-defensive and over-sensitive to the fairest of comments given with a large helping of praise, the fragile nature of her sanity should be borne in mind. She tried to throw herself from a window at the age of fourteen, had been certified technically insane in 1895 and again in 1913, and she had an extra-sensitivity that made her endure agonies when her work was placed before the public for scrutiny.

> *May 11, 1927* My book. What is the use of saying one is indifferent to reviews when positive praise, though mingled with blame, gives one such a start, that instead of feeling dried up, one feels, on the contrary, flooded with ideas . . .

The corollary was a fear, far beyond the ordinary, of adverse criticism. As Quentin Bell reveals in his classic biography of her, five days after the above entry she also wrote: '*May 16, 1927* Suppose one woke and found oneself a fraud? It was part of my madness that horror . . .'

She and Bennett eventually met in person, three months before his death. Her account reveals the blend of snobbery and uncharitableness that was the least attractive side of her, but it also reveals how much she cared for literature:

> *December 2nd, 1930* . . . There I was for 2 hours so it seemed, alone with B, in Ethel's little back room. [Ethel was Ethel Sands] And this meeting I am convinced was engineered by B to 'get on good terms with Mrs. Woolf' – When heaven knows I don't care a rap if I'm on terms with B or not . . .

She adds some details of Bennett's stutter, and goes on '... I like the old creature. I do my best, as a writer, to detect signs of genius in his smoky brown eye'.

She adds some sneers about his methods of working – 'this incessant scribbling, one word after another, one thousand words daily'. (In fact, though a thousand words in a day may have seemed 'an incessant scribble' to her, it would have been a slack day for him, as we have seen.) The evening did not have a happy end, particularly when Bennett was bold enough to teasingly inform Lord David Cecil that he was isolated from life itself in his stately home at Hatfield, and open 'on Thursdays only' to real experience. This, a hint that ivory-tower isolationism might not be the best stance for a writer clearly rankled with her:

> 'And you drop your aitches on purpose', I said, 'thinking that you possess more "life" than we do'. 'I sometimes tease', said B, 'but I don't think I possess more life than you do. Now I must go home. I have to write one thousand words tomorrow morning'. And this left only the scrag end of the evening; and this left me in a state where I can hardly drive my pen across the page.

She was unable to forgive, even when Bennett died. For her, he was an old bore and an egotist, 'much at the mercy of life for all his competence; a shopkeeper's view of literature; yet with the rudiments, covered with fat and prosperity and the desire for hideous Empire furniture'.

One can see what Harold Nicolson meant when he read her diary and recorded in his own:

> There is nothing of her distinction, charm and occasional affection and kindness in her diary. She seems neurotic, vain and envious. But it is fascinating nonetheless ...

Taken in conjunction with that of Bennett, Virginia Woolf's diary could be said to represent one pole of the two extremes of literature, Arnold Bennett's objective search for truth on the one hand, and her own subjective search for an inner reality on the other. That the one school should disintegrate into sloppy pseudo-naturalism, and the other into the portentous and narrow limitations of côterie art should not disguise for us that in Bennett and Woolf both schools found worthy representatives.

In this dichotomy between popular and rarefied art, there is no doubt where our last 'literary' diarist would place himself: he would argue cogently that nothing of any intellectual or spiritual worth could ever be felt by the mob. And because of his own high intelligence and early mental development, he was never really able to identify with the rest of mankind. His main interest throughout his life was the one with which he began, and the only one he thought fundamentally worth his attention: himself. In two books, published under the pseudonym 'Barbellion', *Journal of a Disappointed Man* (1919) and the posthumously published *A Last Diary* (1921), B. F. Cummings, a West London naturalist, put himself on display in as calculated, if more dramatic, a manner as he would have impaled an insect on a pin or turned his microscope on an amoeba. He himself was not a physically healthy specimen. He nearly died of pneumonia as a child and remained under-sized and puny. More seriously, he developed disseminated sclerosis.

From the age of twelve, he began to confide to a diary the thoughts he was incapable of imparting to a sympathetic ear in real life. In his early teens he determined to become a naturalist, and in the early pages of his diary he shows an already formidable knowledge of the natural world, and a precocious ability for dissecting his own motivations. He could never bring himself to mouth the little white lies that eased personal relationships. When he starts to go out with girls, there are callousnesses on his part because their intellects are no match for his, and he has nothing but contempt for any who would live life at less frenzied a level than himself – at a Beethoven concert, for example:

This symphony always works me up into an ecstasy; in ecstatic sympathy with its dreadfulness I could stand up in the balcony and fling myself down passionately into the arena below. Yet there were women sitting alongside me to-day – knitting. It so irritated me that at the end of the first movement I got up and sat elsewhere. They would have sat knitting at the foot of the Cross I suppose.

Perhaps the intensity he demanded from and gave to life stemmed from some sort of subconscious realization that his life would be short. He did marry, but he did so not realizing that he had only a few years to live. His wife, who chose to marry him anyway, *did* know, as he found out later:

She has known *all* from the beginning! M— warned her not to marry me. How brave and loyal of her! What an ass I have been. I am overwhelmed with feelings of shame and self contempt and sorrow for her. She is quite cheerful and an enormous help . . .

That is about the nearest to expressing love for another person that Barbellion came. Normally his reaction was more of the kind '. . . I solemnly thank God that I am not as other men are'.

If diarists ever have a desire to achieve the acclaim of posterity to make up for their lack of recognition in their own time, then Barbellion has this quality. Whatever happens, his diaries must be preserved:

. . . Supposing I lost them I cannot imagine the anguish it would cause me. It would be the death of my real self, and as I should take no pleasure in the perpetuation of my flabby, flaccid, anaemic, amiable, puppet self, I shall probably commit suicide.

He claimed that this was not a matter of wanting immediate acclaim:

Some of my weaknesses I publish, and no doubt you say

at once 'self-advertisement'. I agree more or less, but believe *egotism* is a diagnosis nearer the mark. I do not aspire to Tolstoi's *ethical* motives. Mine are *intellectual*. I am the scientific investigator of myself, and if the published researches bring me into notice, I am not averse from it, though interest in my work comes first.

His reason for writing the above (which comes from the *Last Diary*) is that he had edited and prepared extracts from his diary for publication. At the end of the book, at his insistence, was printed the line: 'Barbellion died on December 31.' Perhaps the reason for this, whatever rationalizations he afterwards made of his action, is that he was determined to have his cake and eat it. He thought ('Reading it through again, I see what a remarkable book I have written') that it would be acclaimed a masterpiece on publication, all the more glorious because the reviewers would be uninhibited by the author being alive. Posthumous fame awarded to someone still living would be confirmation of his suspicions of the world. It did not quite work out like that, but it was near enough the truth.

In October 1919 he did indeed die, at the age of thirty-one, having had to relinquish his post with the British Museum of Natural History in 1917 due to his deteriorating condition. He left behind him the *Last Diary* which was published in 1921. This time the last words of the book were from *Hamlet*: 'The rest is silence.'

Even at the last his intellectual arrogance breaks through. After suffering the physical (welcome) and mental (unwelcome) attentions of a nurse, he writes:

But what a beautifully geometrical Nemesis it all is! Here am I in the last scene of the last act, the ruthless, arrogant intellectual, spending the last days of his ruined life alone, in the close companionship of an uneducated village woman who reads *Answers*.

Yet he can look into the cage in his sickroom and reflect on the similarity between himself and the canary:

> For I, too, silent, concealed in my bed, possess a heart pumping incessantly, though not so fast. I, too, am an animal, little bird, and we must both die . . .

Neither of his diaries is the literary masterpiece he would like to have it thought, but as products of a scientific mind which turned a critical examination upon itself, they remain provocative examinations of an amusing and arrogant personality.

BIBLIOGRAPHY

Mary Shelley's Journal, edited by F. L. Jones (University of Oklahoma Press, 1947).

The Journal of Sir Walter Scott, first published in 1890 by D. Douglas of Edinburgh in two volumes. A number of later editions.

Henry Crabb Robinson: *Diary, Reminiscences and Correspondence of Henry Crabb Robinson*, edited by T. Sadler and published in 3 volumes in 1869. Also *Henry Crabb Robinson on Books and their Writers*, edited by Edith J. Morley in 3 volumes (Dent, 1938).

Letters of George Gissing to Members of his Family, collected and arranged by Algernon and Ellen Gissing (Constable, 1927).

Arnold Bennett: *The Journals of Arnold Bennett*, edited by Newman Flower in 3 volumes (Cassell, 1932–3). Also a one-volume selection by Frank Swinnerton (Penguin Books, number 999, 1954).

Virginia Woolf: *A Writer's Diary*, edited by Leonard Woolf (Hogarth Press, 1953).

W. N. P. Barbellion (B. F. Cummings): *The Journal of a Disappointed Man* (Chatto and Windus, 1919); *A Last Diary* (Chatto and Windus, 1920).

NINE

Whispers from the Corridors of Power

If the diary has been the one companion for a writer in the solitude of the study, it has been no less a confidante of that most gregarious of mortals, the politician. Politicians love gossip, but above all they love confidential gossip, the little secrets that they can hug to their bosoms only to be imparted to the closest of friends 'providing it doesn't go further'. Mostly it does go further, but 'off the record'. The rest of us have usually to wait for years until some political figure retiring from the arena spices his memoirs with the little secrets he was privy to during his time.

If there were to be a rating system for politicians, it might well be on a secrets scale. Small fry are two-secrets men, prominent backbenchers four-secrets men, all the way up to prime ministers, or presidents, who are about ten-secrets men. Unfortunately, the further up what one Conservative ex-minister has called the greasy pole, the more one's capacity to survive depends upon the keeping of secrets. And a few years spent in office, where discretion is vital, begin to breed a my-lips-are-sealed, cards-to-the-chest mentality that affects even retirement. The lips buttoned for so long atrophy, and the long-awaited memoirs have that deadpan impenetrable capacity for uninformative cliché that is the average statesman's stock in trade.

Certain politicians – Lord Butler or Richard Crossman for example – achieve a slight notoriety in their own time for a capacity to say the things more pompous men would prefer unsaid, but there is a conspicuous lack of the really appalling indiscretion that makes the good diarist irresistible. It would be unwise to assume that the day of the political diarist of this kind has gone for ever. Somewhere among 630 members of parliament there is sure to be at least one scribbling away for posterity, a secret recorder of the things prominent men hope will be forgotten.

On the basis of some of the best diaries of the past, it is possible to build an identi-kit picture of what he (or she) will be like. Firstly, he must not be too successful in his own career. Ambition itself is acceptable but not success; if he reaches a nine- or ten-secrets rating, a paralysis engendered by years of 'No comments' will finish him before he has properly begun. Secondly, he must not be so unimportant that no one of import ever speaks to him. Thirdly, if he is a good talker himself it will help to attract unsuspecting potential victims, but he will have to be a good listener too to harvest his gains. Fourthly, he must be congenial enough company to be invited to the dinner parties, country weekends, and London club enclaves where matters of import are *really* decided.

The first political diarist was active during the first half of the eighteenth century, the period which has been termed the Whip supremacy, when the edifying career of Baron Melcombe, better known as George Bubb Dodington, was flourishing. He was born in 1691 just three years after the Glorious Revolution. His name was Bubb and his father an apothecary, but on his maternal side he could claim an uncle George Dodington who compiled a vast fortune under William III and Anne and who furthered his young nephew's career. The borough of Winchelsea being in Uncle George's pocket, young George had only to complete his education to walk into Parliament as Winchelsea's M.P. in 1715 at the politically tender age of twenty-four. Five years later, the uncle obligingly died leaving George a vast pile of ready cash, a life sinecure of an Irish clerkship, and an unfinished palace (by the architect Vanbrugh) in Dorset.

George spent some of the money – £140,000 – on finishing the palace, and, giving credit where credit was due, adopted his uncle's surname to become George Bubb Dodington.

By 1722 he became the Hon. Member for Bridgewater, but more important under the prevailing conditions, he controlled Winchelsea, Weymouth, and Melcombe Regis (which itself returned four M.P.s) as well as his own constituency. With this parcel of votes to deliver to the best offer, he was a man to cultivate. George, however, was not one to wait quietly in the corner to be approached. Rather, he elevated the craft of sycophancy to a minor art form. He began to court Walpole, to whom he addressed obsequious verses, but after a while, to be on the safe side, he courted Frederick, Prince of Wales, and abused Walpole in private. None the less, he followed Walpole to power and served for fifteen years as a Treasury Commissioner, but when it came to the political crisis of 1741–2 he finished up attacking Walpole, who in turn pointed out that George had been quite willing to share his infamy for fifteen years.

In 1744, he became treasurer of the navy under Pelham, but by 1749 he was being privately wooed by the Prince of Wales again, despite the unsteady nature of their relationship in the past. He threw his lot in with the Prince, who promised him a long-coveted peerage, but in 1751 the Prince very inconveniently took it into his head to die before the King.

At the end of the 1740s Dodington had begun to keep a diary, with the intention of justifying himself to posterity; but with a twist of fate as unkind as he deserved, the diary published twenty years after his death was used as a symbol of the corruption of his age, and as a banner to wave in the new cause of reform.

Dodington's first reaction to his secret patron's death was to quit politics: 'I have done enough and henceforth shall live to myself the years which God in his mercy grant me unless I am called upon to assist . . .'

By now he had a villa at Hammersmith, as well as his country home, 'A monument of tasteless splendour' it was once called, and it would have been easy for him to eke out a quiet and wealthy retirement there. That, though, was not in character. He needed to feel important. Again he tried playing both ends against the middle. He joined the bereaved Princess in attacking Pelham, but at the same time wooed Pelham for any services likely to be rendered.

> I was come to offer him not only that [i.e. a favourable result at Weymouth] but all the services in my power, and that I was authoris'd to say the same from all my friends . . .

Pelham, however, also died before George could properly reap rewards, and he had to transfer his suits to Newcastle! ('That I was come, to assure him of my most dutiful affection, and sincere attachment to him, simply, having no engagements to make me look to the right or the left . . .') Unfortunately, Dodington's attempts to hold the Bridgewater constituency for Newcastle failed and he lost out to Lord Egmont. When the voice of the people spoke, in the shape of constituents, his reaction was the scathing observation that the voters displayed 'infamous and disagreeable compliance with the low habits of venal wretches'. He sat for Weymouth instead and continued his intrigues, meanwhile assuring Newcastle that no expense had been spared at Bridgewater. At the end of 1755, the effort paid off:

> *December 17th* I went to Newcastle House. With much assurances of confidential friendship, the D. told me that he had the King's leave to offer me the Treasury of the Navy: which I accepted.

The job lasted less than a year:

> *November 16th, 1756* Went to Devonshire House – The Duke told me that he was forc'd by the King to take the

employment he held – That he was order'd to go to Mr.
Pitt and know upon what conditions he would serve –
That in the arrangements he and his friends made, my
office was demanded. He was very sorry – had no hand
in it – Behav'd very civilly & c.

Whatever sins can be laid at his door, lack of staying
power was not one of them. He held office again briefly,
until ousted for a second time at Pitt's behest. But in 1761,
an eager parasite to the last, the new choice of host to his
activities, Lord Bute, turned up trumps with his long-
awaited peerage. The next year he died, the most unashamed
political place-hunter of them all.

If Dodington had lived to witness the 'great divide'
between the old-style politics and the new, drawn by the
Reform Bill of 1832, he would perhaps have felt like a pre-
historic monster whose natural habitat had been changed
completely, therefore dooming the animal, because of its
inability to adapt, to extinction. However, another political
diarist, though launched into politics when aristocratic
influence was all, and sinecures divided up like spoils, was
sufficiently intelligent and perceptive (despite his strong
disapproval of such popular manifestations as the Chartists)
to be able to regard the coming of the new regime with a
patrician ease.

Charles Cavendish Fulke Greville (1794–1865) was a
diarist for about fifty years of his life, leaving behind him
ninety-three notebooks. They were entrusted to his friend
Henry Reeve with publication in mind, at least for 'such
proportions of them as might be thought of public interest
whenever that could be done without inconvenience to
living persons'. When Reeve published a first selection of
extracts in 1865, another prolific diarist, Queen Victoria,
found the 'proportions' chosen not to her liking: 'DIS-
GRACEFULLY *Bad taste* . . . the tone in which it speaks
of Royalty is . . . most reprehensible!' Similarly, it was
Greville that Lord Rosebery had in mind when he said:

I have a holy horror of a diarist, a man who feels bound to write something and makes a confidante of his journal is subject to every human meanness ...

Greville had his reasons for keeping a diary. Occasionally he says he will give it up as 'foolish and unprofitable', but normally he is true to his declared intention:

As I don't write history I omit to note such facts as are recorded in the newspapers and merely mention the odd things I pick up which are not generally known and which may throw some light on those which are ...

and, perhaps, to a rather different stimulus: 'I find relief by giving vent on paper to that which I cannot say to anybody ...' What makes Greville's diaries an outstandingly important source of information about the politics of the first half of the nineteenth century is his intention to throw light on the unknown and the 'odd', but what makes them such a pleasure to read is the balance and dignified style of his prose, to say nothing of the indiscretion. He was not impressed by Fanny Burney's diaries:

They are overlaid with an enormous quantity of trash and twaddle and there is a continuous stream of mawkish sentimentality, loyalty, devotion, sensibility and a display of feelings and virtues which are very provoking ...

But it was not this type of attack which upset the Queen. It was his appalling capacity to tell the truth about her recently departed relatives:

... The King [i.e. William IV] has been to Woolwich, inspecting the artillery, to whom he gave a dinner, with toasts and hip, hip, hurrahing, and three times three, himself giving the time. I tremble for him; at present he is only a mountebank but he bids fair to be a maniac ...
... After dinner he made a number of speeches, so ridiculous and so nonsensical, beyond all belief but to

those who heard them, rambling from one subject to another repeating the same thing over and over again and altogether such a mass of confusion, trash, and imbecility as made one blush and laugh at the same time . . .

. . . If he was not such an ass that nobody does anything but laugh at what he says, this would be very important. Such as he is, it is nothing. 'What can you expect' (as I forget who said) 'from a man with a head like a pine apple'. His head is just of that shape.

The surviving children of George III were not the monarchy's greatest advertisement:

Good God, what a set they are! . . . We talked over the Royal Family, and we agreed that the three Kingdoms cannot furnish such a brood, so many and so bad, rogues, blackguards, fools and whores . . .

The so-called intellectual leaders of thought and manners did not escape his sharp attention either. Macaulay, for example:

Not a ray of intellect beams from his countenance . . . His figure, face, voice, manner are all bad; he astonishes and instructs, he seldom entertains, seldom amuses, and still seldomer pleases. He wants variety, elasticity, gracefulness; his is a roaring torrent, and not a meandering stream of talk.

Greville's own career is worth examination. Just as Dodington had a head start by virtue of his family connections, so did Greville – born into one of the oldest families in the country (his grandfather, the Duke of Portland, was twice Prime Minister). At this time, any government post was a lucrative source of revenue to the incumbent and therefore subject to all sorts of wheelings, dealings, and 'inheritings'. Greville obtained reversions (i.e. the right to succeed to an office when it became vacant) to two posts: Secretary to the Island of Jamaica, and Clerk Extraordinary to the Privy Council. The first reversion was obtained in 1801 and the second in 1804, when Greville was seven and ten years old respectively – such practice was typical of the system prevailing at the time. Although he left Christ Church, Oxford without a degree, he eventually succeeded to both these posts. He also became private secretary to Earl Bathurst, the Secretary of State for War, and in 1821 Clerk to the Privy Council. It was this latter post which brought him into contact with everyone who mattered, from whom he learned the many secrets he was to impart to readers decades later.

He remained a bachelor all his life: his real passion was horse-racing, though the Turf was an addiction he some-times tried to break. (On one occasion, Greville's lack of discretion let him down on the course. He was in partner-ship with Lord George Bentinck for a few years. Together they owned Preserve which won the 1835 One Thousand Guineas and was expected to win The Oaks. Greville gave the riding instructions to their jockey in the hearing of a rival trainer, who countered them with some of his own. Losses, particularly on Lord George's part, were heavy, and cordiality was never restored between Greville and Lord George thereafter.)

He was one of the oldest members of the Jockey Club, once won £14,000 on the Derby, and he owned a St Leger winner. It is not as a racing man, however, that he has gone down in history but as perhaps the greatest political diarist of all time – the man who took advantage of his special position to tell posterity the truth as he saw it. What more could we reasonably ask of him?

With the passing of Greville, or perhaps the publication of Greville, journals began to take on a different tone. The solemn and dedicated approach to public life prevalent in the Victorian era did not lend itself to the classic behind-the-scenes diary, but in the twentieth century, something of the quality of Greville's life is recaptured in *Lloyd George: a diary*, by Frances Stevenson, which provides an appraisal of a major political figure from the standpoint of his secretary and mistress. The most loved and the most hated of politicians, Lloyd George was a mass of contradictions: a champion of the masses surrounded by the rich and well-born; an opponent of one war who advocated wholesale slaughter in the next; a champion of liberalism who wrecked the Liberal Party; a castigator of the misuse of power who sold honours – how could an account of life with such a man fail to be fascinating? The diarist herself was first employed by Lloyd George in 1911 as a summer tutor for his daughter Megan. Later she was invited to join him at the Treasury (he was Chancellor of the Exchequer from 1908–15), though he made it clear this would be not only a business relationship but one Frances Stevenson describes as being 'on his own terms, which were in direct conflict with my essentially Victorian upbringing'.

Not only was Frances Stevenson in a privileged position, by the side of the most interesting political figure of the day, but she was, moreover, an intelligent, well-educated woman in her own right. As the editor of the diary, A. J. P. Taylor, has said, what makes her account even more interesting on occasion is that she records not what happens in cabinet, etc., but what Lloyd George *says* happened in cabinet.

What will appeal to those readers without a historian's or a politician's interest in the events is that hers is a particularly human story too. She tried to give the Welsh Wizard the home life and love that his own marriage lacked, and she stayed with him when it would have been infinitely easier to opt out of so ambiguous a position. She records both the facts and the feelings but she never indulges in self-pity.

January 17th, 1915 . . . C.[1] returned from Wales on Dec

---

[1] At this stage Frances Stevenson refers to Lloyd George as 'C' (for Chancellor); later she calls him 'D' (for David).

29th and from then till now I have been with him at W.H. [Walton Heath, where Lloyd George had a house in addition to the one at home in Wales] coming up every day to town, & going back in the evening. It has been like an idyll, but alas! came to an end yesterday, when the family returned from Criccieth, and I returned home . . .

Several insights into Lloyd George's motivations are recorded in his words:

'. . . I think it was Victor Hugo's book Les Misérables that decided me to do what I could to alleviate the distress and suffering of the poor . . . a great many people think it was because I was born and lived among poor people that I turned my mind to reforms & schemes for alleviating want & suffering. But they are mistaken . . . there was no *wretchedness* in our district. The homes that you might think poor I used to look on as comfortable – homes where they used to have cake, and treacle on their bread – luxuries which we children rarely enjoyed! But I never saw any of privation & suffering which is depicted in Les Misérables. It was not until I grew up and left Wales that I realised what poverty really meant and what a need the poor have of someone to fight for them . . .'

Another literary work also influenced him strongly:

. . . C says that Ibsen's Doll's House was the work that converted him to woman suffrage, & presented the woman's point of view to him . . .

There are many examples, too, of Lloyd George scoring off his opponents, though none of them scoring off him, but Miss Stevenson is capable of sharp judgments herself: 'Of all the Cabinet worms, I think Montagu is the wormiest . . .'

Of his Conservative opponents (with the exception of Bonar Law, whom she liked), after the to-ings and fro-ings over the premiership in 1916, she writes acidly:

... They were actually kept waiting ten minutes or ¼ of an hour – all these great Tories – Curzon, Cecil & the rest, who a few years ago would not have shaken hands with him & who could find no words strong enough to express their bitterness and hatred – now waiting to be granted an audience of the Little Welsh attorney!

Some memorable anecdotes are also recorded. Lloyd George was fond of golf but did not play the game on Sundays because 'I mustn't shock my Nonconformist friends on too many points at the same time'. A planned game for a Saturday morning was placed in jeopardy when the King suggested an audience at the Palace. 'Damn the King!' said Lloyd George, but when a subterfuge had been resorted to and the audience postponed to Monday, he changed his expletive to 'God bless His Majesty!'.

A nice exchange took place between the monarch and his premier when the King expressed alarm at the news that Lloyd George would have occasion to meet Lenin and Trotsky at a 1922 conference in Genoa. Lloyd George reminded the King that on official duties he had already had to entertain Sami Bey, who had been missing for an entire day only to be traced to an East End house of sodomy, and that Bey was in any case the representative of Mustapha Kemal (who had tired of women and taken to unnatural sexual intercourse). Lloyd George pointed out that there was little to choose between receiving such guests and meeting Lenin, to which the King had no reply but to roar with laughter.

Frances Stevenson's position remained difficult:

D. returned from W.H. very fit after weekend, though we had both been very miserable without each other. D. said he would have sent for me, only that he felt it would not quite be playing the game with Mrs. L.G. 'She is very tolerant' he said 'considering that she knows everything that is going on. It is not right to try her too far.'

It is gratifying to know that she did eventually become Lloyd George's second wife. After his years in office, the diary slackens and fades to nothing in accordance with Lloyd George's career, but as an insight to a man under the pressures of a supreme office, it is a fine document.

Beatrice Webb, though she never entered Parliament, never held office, and played merely the background role of hostess and wife when her husband was in the Cabinet, was a formidable force in politics. She was a diarist throughout her long life, becoming more and more compulsive towards the end, and was in every way a remarkable woman. She grew up as Beatrice Potter in an atmosphere of affluence and intellect. Her father was once Chairman of the Great Western Railway, and her mother wrote political essays and lectures and was an enthusiastic supporter of the anti-Corn-Law campaign. (No less a figure than John Bright called Beatrice's mother 'one of the two or three women a man remembers to the end of his life as beautiful in expression and form'.) The young Beatrice grew up in a home where men like John Bright and Herbert Spencer were regular callers, and as there seemed to be a vogue, during the 1870s and 1880s, for unmarried daughters to dabble in social work of some description, it was perhaps natural that she should be attracted to working among the poor and needy. She assessed applicants for relief in their homes in Soho, London, she collected rents for Octavia Hill, and she even disguised herself as a 'Miss Jones' to help Charles Booth's investigations into the evils of sweating (an episode of her life which provided her friend Bernard Shaw with the outline of a similar scene in *The Millionairess*).

In the course of her activities, she met Sidney Webb and married him in 1892. Together they were instrumental in guiding a whole revolution in British politics, doing more than perhaps anyone else to create opportunities for the Labour Party to rise to power from nothing in a few decades. They were social investigators without parallel, producing exhaustive studies on local government, trade unionism, and kindred matters; they were also responsible for the founding of the London School of Economics, and for the famous report on minorities which finally killed the old Poor Law and cleared the way for more humane methods of relieving destitution.

I stress these facets of Beatrice Webb's career because, mainly at the instigation of her nephew Mr Malcolm Muggeridge, there seems to be a modern tendency to sneer at her, and to regard her as a foolish old woman who spent her entire life preparing herself to grovel to, and fawn on, Soviet Russia. It may legitimately be asked whose activities, the nephew's or the aunt's, have been the more valuable.

Her diaries, which begin in 1869, were used as the basis for two autobiographical works, *My Apprenticeship* and *Our Partnership*, which took her story up to 1911. She was never able to do the same for the later years, so extracts from the diaries have been published since for the remaining years, 1912–24, and 1924–32. We have no less an authority than Samuel Hynes to tell us also that:

A reading of the unpublished diaries at the London School of Economics confirms the sense that one gets from *My Apprenticeship*, that there is an even finer book to come, and that when the full text is published Mrs. Webb will take her place among the great diarists . . .

He has argued, I am sure with some justice, that she was a frustrated novelist who submerged her own natural style to the flat academic prose of Sidney in their joint projects, but who could not suppress it in her diary. He quotes a 1913 entry: 'I never write, except in this diary, in my own style, always in a hybrid of his and mine . . .'

Her attitude to the reading, and by implication to the writing, of fiction was demonstrated by an entry in her diary made long before she met Sidney:

I am quite confident that the education of girls is very

much neglected in the way of their reading . . . the object of reading is to gain knowledge. A novel now and then is a mere recreation to be offered to a growing mind, it cultivates the imagination, but taken as the continued nourishment, it destroys many a young mind . . .

This passage would seem to show that we can hardly lay at Sidney's door the suppression of any instincts she had as a novelist. Is it not rather the case of the young lady, born with every advantage, who needed to assuage her guilt in face of other people's lack of fortune, by dedicating her life to the service of others? She used her own private income to finance the Webb's mammoth research projects, and worked her entire life on behalf of others. Her marriage to Sidney might be seen in the same terms, for she recorded her first impressions in her diary:

. . . at once repulsive and ridiculous. His tiny tadpole body, unhealthy skin, lack of manner, cockney pronunciation and poverty were all against him . . .

Much of the fascination in her published diaries is this capacity to pin down characteristics of her contemporaries. In view of the defection from Labour of Ramsay MacDonald in 1931, her gift for observation lends considerable weight to this entry from 1924:

. . . the P.M. is playing-up – without any kind of consultation with the majority of his colleagues or scruple or squeamishness about first pronouncements – towards the formation of a Centre Party – far less definitely Socialist in home affairs, far less distinctly pacifist in foreign affairs . . . MacDonald wants 8 million votes behind him and means to get them even if this entails shedding the ILP . . . That ladder will be kicked down! . . . he is attracting, by his newly-won prestige and personal magnetism, the Conservative Collectivist element . . . I do not accuse him of treachery; for he was never a Socialist; either revolutionary like Lansbury or administrative like the Webbs ... Where he lacked integrity is in *posing* as a Socialist, and occasionally using revolutionary jargon ...

Her own admiration of the Labour Party stopped a good way short of idolatry, as she shows when returning to the theme of Ramsay MacDonald in August 1926:

> My general impression is that J.R.M. feels himself to be *the* indispensable leader of a new political party which is bound to come into office within his lifetime – a correct forecast I think ... Ramsay MacDonald is not distinguished either in intellect of character, and he has some very mean traits in his nature. But he has great gifts as a political leader, he has personal charm, he has vitality, he is assiduous, self-controlled and skilful. In all these respects he is unique in the inner circle of the Labour Party made up, as it is, of fanatics, faddists, refined and self-effacing intellectuals and the dull mediocrities of the Trade Union Movement ... Ramsay MacDonald is a magnificent substitute for a leader ...

One can sense the change in her diary as the euphoria induced by Labour's first opportunity to form a government in 1924 dissipated in internal and external failures and disappointments:

> Uncle Arthur [Henderson] was bursting with childish joy over his H.O. seals in a red leather box which he handed round the company ... they were all laughing over Wheatley – the revolutionary – going down on both knees and actually kissing the King's hand; and C. P. Trevelyan was remarking that the King seemed quite incapable of saying two words to his new ministers: 'he went through the ceremony like an automaton' ... Altogether we were a jolly party – all laughing at the joke of Labour in Office ...

She was contemptuous of the new Labour ministers'

anxiety to win the approval of the Civil Service, very
unsympathetic to the ill-conceived General Strike of 1926,
and by 1927 had lost much of her interest in the fate of
the party for which she had done so much: 'Deficient in
brains and starved in money, it is a miracle that the Labour
Party steadily grows in voting power . . .'

Crossing the floor, so to speak, to look at a Conservative
diary, the outlooks of the Liberal Lloyd George and the
Labour Mrs Webb may be politically balanced by the
opinions of Sir Henry Channon. Known almost universally
as 'Chips', he was born in 1897 and died in 1958. Though
his diaries for 1918 and for 1923–8 are extant, they remain
unpublished, so this account inevitably relies on the one-
volume edition of his diaries covering the later years
1934–53, edited by Robert Rhodes James. Sir Henry had
his own views on diary-keeping:

> Although I am not Clerk to the Council like Mr. Greville,
> nor Secretary to the Admiralty like Mr. Pepys, nor yet
> 'duc et pair' as was M. de St. Simon, I have, neverthe-
> less, had interesting opportunities of intimacy with
> interesting people and have often been at the centre of
> things . . .

On another occasion, he wrote, 'What is more dull than a
discreet diary? One might just as well have a discreet soul';
to which he added two years later: 'the weaknesses of one's
friends are more amusing to chronicle than their dignified
conduct, which one takes for granted . . .'

He is, of course, absolutely right on all counts. He was a
born diarist and because he was both in Parliament (having
married Lord Iveagh's daughter he succeeded his mother-
in-law to the Southend constituency) and a member of a
top social circle, he was privy to much that others missed,
particularly throughout the unfolding of the Abdication
crisis. One could write pages on his faults – his snobbery,
his lack of awareness of how others live ('It is very difficult
to spend less than £200 a morning when one goes shop-

ping . . .'), his admirations ('I am nuts about Chamberlain . . .') and his ardent support of less-than-admirable
men like Franco, but one would still have to come down
to the fact that he was not unaware of his own faults:

> Sometimes I think I have an unusual character – able
> but trivial; I have flair, intuition, great good taste but
> only second rate ambition: I am far too susceptible to
> flattery; I hate and am uninterested in all the things most
> men like such as sport, business, statistics, debates,
> speeches, war and the weather; but I am rivetted by lust,
> furniture, glamour and society and jewels. I am an
> excellent organiser and have a will of iron; I can only be
> appealed to through my vanity . . .

Some of his determination to cut a dash in London society
certainly stemmed from the fact that he was an American
who loved England but detested America ('The more I
know of American civilization the more I despise it . . .')
and the more he advanced in London society, the better he
felt, showing inordinate pride in having Royalty at his
dinner-table.

His diary will probably be quoted by future historians as
the perfect example of the official party-line Conservative
of the 1930s, pro-Franco, pro-appeasement, and deeply
suspicious of Eden and Churchill. (He was very feline about
Baldwin too – 'He would not have flown to Berchtesgaden
– not he. He wouldn't have known where it was.') Certainly his enthusiasm for Neville Chamberlain could hardly
have been exceeded. Witness his most dramatic account of
the scene in the House of Commons when Chamberlain
announced his plan to fly to meet Hitler at Munich next
day:

> . . . I felt sick with enthusiasm, longed to clutch him –
> he continued for a word or two and then the House
> rose and in a scene of riotous delight, cheered, bellowed
> their approval. We stood on our benches, waved our

order papers, shouted – until we were hoarse – a scene
of indescribable enthusiasm – Peace must now be saved,
and with it the world . . . I will always remember little
Neville today, with his too long hair, greying at the
sides, his smile, his amazing spirits and seeming lack of
fatigue, as he stood there, alone fighting the dogs of
war single-handed and triumphant – he seemed the
reincarnation of St. George – so simple and so unspoilt
. . . I don't know what this country has done to deserve
him.

What the country had done to deserve Chamberlain was
later asked in other senses, and those who got on their
feet and cheered that day did their best to forget it later.
It is the strength of diaries in general, and this one in
particular, that we are given the genuine feelings of the
moment, not the apologetics of a later date.

After the War, men like Chips were a rarer breed. He still
had a sharp eye for the world and its inhabitants. The Royal
Wedding presents (for the then Princess Elizabeth and her
husband-to-be, the Duke of Edinburgh) were 'ghastly',
Aneurin Bevan was 'dreadful', Cripps was 'the modern
Savonarola', Gaitskell had 'a Wykehamistical voice and
manner and a thirteenth-century face', and Ernest Marples
was an 'alert, able, squirrel-like urchin'. He was also able
to compare the 1953 Coronation scene in Westminister
Abbey with that of 1937; both accounts make good reading. He has a good story of a divorced peer concerned
whether he will still be welcome at the 1953 ceremony in
the Abbey despite his changed marital status, and being
reassured by the Earl Marshal: 'Of course you will; this is
the Coronation, not Ascot!'

Chips knew that a rival diarist lurked on the political
fringes in the shape of author and parliamentarian Harold
Nicolson, but the thought did not worry him:

November 15th, 1947 . . . At dinner we discussed diaries,
and Willy [i.e. W. Somerset Maugham] volunteered that

mine would be illuminating. Other diarists he said, would be too cautious; that Eddie Marsh was too kind, and that Harold Nicolson was not in society . . .

Harold Nicolson's diaries, together with the letters which passed between himself and Vita Sackville-West, his wife, have been published in three volumes edited by Nigel Nicolson, their son. Harold Nicolson had rather different views from Chips on diary-keeping, which he expressed at various times:

December 28th, 1941 . . . I do a *Spectator* article on keeping diaries, in which I lay down the rule that one should write one's diary for one's great-grandson. I think that is a correct rule. The purely private diary becomes too self-centered and morbid. One should have a remote, but not too remote, audience.

November 9th, 1947 Read Arthur Bryant on Pepys. It is odd how the English love a man who is not a humbug like themselves. To my mind Pepys was a mean little man. Salacious in a grubby way; even in his peculations there was no magnificence. But he did stick in his office during the Plague, which was more than most men did. It is some relief to reflect that to be a good diarist one must have a little snouty sneaky mind.

January 3rd, 1953 James [i.e. James Pope-Hennessy] says that my diary is too boring for words and that there is no use going on with it . . . He thinks no diary is of any value unless it expresses personal opinions, feelings, and gossip, and recounts all that is said . . . I do not think it right to record day by day all the turpitude or sexual aberrations of my friends. I love them too dearly for that.

These are not the philosophies which produce great diaries. The very urbanity and charitableness of Harold Nicolson are against him in matching Pepys or even Chips in the art of revealing in a diary the indiscreet secrets unconfided elsewhere. He intended his diaries to be for publication, but unlike Chips he allowed this to inhibit his approach. He is usually diffident, rarely intimate, and his discretion is the sign of a trained diplomat who relinquished the salary but not the protocol when he resigned from the Foreign Office at the age of forty-four.

If, however, his natural diffidence belongs to the debit side of the balance, there is still a great deal to place on the plus side. He is never malicious, he is perceptive, he is sensitive, he is often 'in the know', and if there are times when he can be politically naïve, there are others when he flatly refuses to be swept away by the emotions of the moment. While Chips and his friends were cheering and waving their order papers, Harold Nicolson (who had associated himself with the anti-Chamberlain group of Eden, Duff Cooper, Macmillan, Boothby, and Sandys), was one of the few with the courage to remain seated.

He was, one supposes, a natural aristocrat and Conservative, who never found his rightful political place. He had sufficient talent for a distinguished political career but if it is true, as President Truman said, that the man who cannot stand the heat should stay out of the kitchen, then Harold Nicolson was naturally fated to be left in the dining-room waiting for someone else to bring him the food. When it was not forthcoming and he had to fend for himself, he did not lack for moral courage, but his natural fastidiousness made him congenitally incapable of coping with the situation, and he would finish up with a sad and sorry meal for himself.

It started in 1931. With Conservative, Liberal and Labour Parties to choose from (none of whom, one hazards, would have demanded too great a sacrifice of his existing principles), Nicolson joined Oswald Mosley's ill-fated New Party. He left it again before it plummeted to its full quota of Fascism, but it was still not the most perceptive of choices. When he left Beaverbrook's *Evening Standard* to edit Mosley's paper *Action*, he wrote:

I have learnt that shallowness is the supreme evil. I have learnt that rapidity, hustle and rush are the allies of superficiality. My fastidiousness has been increased and with it a loathing of the uneducated. I have come to believe that the gulf between the educated and the uneducated is wider than that between the classes and more galling to the opposite side . . .

A month later Mosley was attacked at a New Party meeting in Glasgow at which a brawl broke out:

> . . . We have a meeting of the Party. Tom says that this forces us to be fascist and that we need no longer hesitate to create our trained and disciplined force. We discuss their uniforms. I suggest grey flannel trousers and shirts.

Is there not something symbolic about the choice – Nicolson's natural reticence causing him to opt for grey instead of the more sinister black that Mosley was to make all too familiar for the rest of the decade?

Beaten heavily as a New Party candidate at the 1931 election, he opted out of the New Party four months later and was out of politics for a few years until the General Election of 1935 when he was persuaded, though the persuasion seems to have been minimal, to stand at Leicester as a National Labour candidate. A man whose vision of England was that seen from, in the words of his son and editor, 'the world of weekend parties, exclusive luncheons, Bloomsbury and the Travellers Club', did not take kindly to the hustings. His dislike for the electors was only marginally ameliorated by their sending him to Westminster for the next ten years. At least posterity gained, by virtue of his diary, from his presence at the heart of national affairs. And his diary gains in significance with his day-by-day accounts of the Abdication crisis, and the anti-Government movements of 1937–8.

A recurring refrain in the diaries is the general futility of the working classes, lying as they did outside the narrow world of the diarist, as indeed did the other groups he disliked – Americans, Jews, women and blacks, for example.

> I believe that our lower classes are for some curious reason congenitally indolent, and that only the pressure of gain or destitution makes them work. When their profits are taken for income tax and they are insured against destitution, their natural indolence comes to the surface . . .

The general triumph of the choice of those lower classes in 1945 elected a Labour Government with a large majority – it also cost Nicolson his seat. He was now faced with another political dilemma. He wanted to retain his membership of that congenial London club at Westminster, but shrank from paying the necessary 'subscription' of successfully appealing to the electorate to put him there. A peerage would have been the answer, but there was a snag there too: patronage was now in the hands of the successful Labour Party, and they were inclined to send to the Lords only men who would support them. After some considerable heart-searching, he joined the Labour Party. He also accepted the Labour candidature at a Croydon by-election in 1948. The by-election and his campaign, which he hated, were twin disasters for him and his new party, and he was left to ruminate on another bad political decision: 'I fear my Socialism is purely cerebral; I do not like the masses in the flesh . . .' Two years later, when he had read the party manifesto for the 1950 election, he reflected:

> How I wish I had not been such an impulsive fool as to join the Labour Party. It was certainly the cardinal error of my life. But I cannot redeem it now . . .

'Chips' in *his* diary recorded the Croydon result:

> . . . that nice silly Harold Nicolson was the worst candidate within human memory . . . his ridiculous behaviour as the Labour candidate . . .

Chips has probably put his finger on it. Throughout his diaries, Nicolson comes over as nice, silly Harold – incapable of dissembling to potential constituents, but incapable of dissembling to his diary either. It made him a political failure, but the same quality made him a very considerable diarist with a capacity to reveal himself more than he perhaps ever realized.

How Harold Nicolson would have disliked the published diary of Cecil King! How Charles Greville and Chips might have revelled in it! Until a boardroom revolution, Mr King was head of the I.P.C. publishing group, controllers of the *Daily Mirror* and other publications, and he claimed that his diary 'was written out of interest and with no thought of publication ... My method ... is to jot down what strikes me as interesting on the day it happens – or at latest the following day ...'.

He takes, he tells us, the stance of 'a privileged and experienced observer with no axe to grind'. One can only assume this is because the axe had never been allowed to get blunt for, in the diary, he uses it on Mr Harold Wilson and others with some purpose. Mr King explains that his own efforts with the *Daily Mirror* swung the balance in favour of Labour at the 1964 General Election, the electorate obediently going to the polls and voting as the *Mirror* told them. Unfortunately they voted for a lot of men for whom Cecil King had scant respect, and who consistently failed to come up to the high standards he had set. This applied to men like Frank Soskice – 'ill and slowly seizing up'; Frank Longford – 'quite useless – mental age of twelve'; Michael Stewart – 'a man so dim as almost to be invisible'; Anthony Crosland – 'immature and quite silly at times'; James Callaghan – 'very nice but has neither the brains nor the education to grasp the problems of the Treasury'. The alternative choice of Lord Home particularly failed to appeal to Mr King – 'I said he would make a good vice-chairman of a sub-committee of the Berwickshire County Council'.

Harold Wilson, after taking office, also began to lose Mr King's esteem, proving himself a man of 'quite astonishing vanity', a quality particularly upsetting to so modest a man as Mr King.

Unfortunately, Cecil King's colleagues at the *Daily Mirror* did not quite appreciate his attempts to put government and country back on the straight and narrow path, and they sacked him in May 1968. He 'rang up the BBC News and ITN and told them I was dismissed and wished to appear on the six o'clock news'. The nation took the news more calmly than could be expected, but that might well have been because they knew the sacking would give Mr King more time to sit down to lunch with Lord Robens and Lord Shawcross and work out a coalition Cabinet to save the country.

With the experience behind him of using print and television to tear the elected government to bits, Mr King was at some pains to explain to his potential allies that this sort of thing could not go on:

> I argued that there will have to be a censorship board; you cannot have everyone in print, on TV and on the stage tearing society to bits. The old cry was 'Liberty not Licence'. Now we have licence and the only way back is a curtailment of liberty.

He was also now free to drift around the world interviewing important and busy statesmen which helped him to form the further opinion that 'the idea of letting insignificant M.P.s drift around the world . . . interviewing important and busy statesmen is rather alarming'. Indeed, one can see that those answerable to their party and to the electorate at every election can hardly expect to be trusted with the same sort of privileges as forcibly retired newspaper proprietors answerable to no one. The diary reveals too that Mr King found King Faisal the most impressive political figure he had ever met. If only those who controlled our destinies were capable of so acute an assessment of a man's worth, Mr

King would not languish in neglect, a millenarian without an audience, but would be given some government post where his charm, modesty and discretion would be better appreciated.

BIBLIOGRAPHY

The Political Journal of George Bubb Dodington, edited by John Carswell and Lewis Arnold Dralle (Clarendon Press, Oxford, 1965).

Charles Greville: *The Greville Memoirs 1814–1860*, edited by Lytton Strachey and Roger Fulford in 8 volumes (Macmillan, 1938).

Frances Stevenson: *Lloyd George: a diary*, edited by A. J. P. Taylor (Hutchinson, 1971).

Beatrice Webb's Diaries 1912–1924, edited by Margaret Cole (Longmans, 1952); *Beatrice Webb's Diaries 1924–1932* edited by Margaret Cole (Longmans, 1956).

Sir Henry Channon: *Chips: the Diaries of Sir Henry Channon*, edited by Robert Rhodes James (Weidenfeld and Nicolson, 1967; Penguin Books, 1970).

Sir Harold Nicolson: *Diaries and Letters*, edited by Nigel Nicolson in 3 volumes (Collins, 1966–8).

Cecil H. King: *The Cecil King Diary 1965–70* (Cape, 1972).

TEN

The Female of the Species

Devoting a chapter specifically to women diarists may seem a trifle reactionary, implying that women are a special breed, capable of acting only in a peculiarly feminine manner and unable to enjoy the diversity of experience that their male counterparts reveal in their writings. It is akin to saying that women are incapable of behaving like politicians or authors, but continually demonstrate the perplexing if predictable peculiarities of the female mind. This would be of course utter nonsense. Women diarists come from every field of human endeavour and their diaries are as entertaining and informative as any written by their male companions. Yet despite this undoubted literary equality of the men and women who have kept diaries, there is still something to be said for considering the woman's diary as a specific subject.

In our own age, when a new and more widespread consciousness is developing amidst the distaff portion of the population, it cannot fail to be of interest to see how the role of women in society has changed over the past three centuries. As women today fight for equality of opportunity, parity in wages, and to create a social environment more fitting to their untapped resources, the plight of the woman of the past takes on a greater significance. How did she cope with the restrictions relentlessly imposed by a male-dominated society, and how was she able to make a life for herself which did not completely frustrate her creative potential?

For those seeking the answers to such questions, the diary becomes an important piece of historical evidence. Firstly, it reveals women who were articulate, and who held opinions on many facets of society. Secondly, it provided a sympathetic ear for women to confide opinions which might have been considered too outrageous for the society they lived in. In the days when the term 'women's rights' was used only by courageous women prepared to be ostracized by society, or as an excuse for political and social abuse, the diaries of women reveal a growing ferment which was to explode with the Edwardian suffragettes and the women's liberationists of our own day.

It is not that the women's diaries of the past are exclusively concerned with the plight of women or the necessity for change. Some are merely records of the day-to-day existence of women raising families and tending to the household chores. Yet even these diaries, with their wealth of domestic trivia, give us a graphic record of what it was like to be a middle- or upper-class woman in former times, and show how their existence differed from and in some cases paralleled that of many women today. It is hardly necessary to add that the total lack of educational and social opportunity for working-class women made them, in terms of the journal as well as the ballot box, the larger and more silent majority.

The seventeenth century, which yielded a host of diaries, includes one of the most interesting – that of Mary Woodforde, wife of Samuel, an eminent gentleman and a Fellow of the Royal Society. Mary's diary is but one of the many Woodforde diaries which were kept by the family and which reveal the changing of attitudes and circumstances among the various generations. Mary's diary, running from the end of November 1684 until June 1690, shows her private concerns as her family is educated and grows up, and the public changes in England as James II is deposed to be replaced in 1689 by William of Orange.

Born Mary Norton of Binstead in Hampshire, she became Mrs Samuel Woodforde, mistress of the Manor of Westcotte in 1667, the very year in which her husband was installed as prebendary of Chichester. Samuel, an active and energetic man, was made a Doctor of Divinity by the Archbishop of Canterbury in 1668 and his book *Paraphrase upon the Psalms* (1679), which included some of his own secular poetry, made him something of a reputation in clerical circles. He had been educated at St Paul's School and from there became a Commoner at Wadham College, Oxford. In 1661, he had married his first wife, Alice Beale, who died giving birth to their second child three years later. In the same year he inherited from an uncle the Manor of Westcotte near Binstead in Hampshire and it was in Binstead that he met his second wife Mary. Better educated than the average cleric of the day himself, he made sure that his children were also given the intellectual equipment to interpret the word of God.

In 1684, when Mary's diary opens, Samuel's eldest son Heighes is twenty and has recently matriculated at Wadham College, Oxford, his father's old college. Five other Woodforde children are mentioned in the diaries – Samuel's second son, Samuel, who goes to St John's College, Cambridge, the third, son, John, who is at school at Winchester and who in 1689 goes to New College, Oxford, and the two youngest boys who attend a Mr Wallace's school in Winchester. The daughter, Alice, was naturally spared such mental rigours and we can detect a distinct note of relief in Mary's diary when she expresses her happiness at her daughter's marriage. Her delight at the marriage of Heighes to Mary Lamport of Alton is just as genuine and the prayers she records for the couple's happiness just as sincere, but underlying the respective entries is the knowledge that the opportunities for Heighes as a bachelor had been infinitely wider than those of Alice as a spinster.

Mary Woodforde was a religious woman in a religious age, but the entries in her diary are concerned less with theological and doctrinal matters than with the spiritual welfare of her family and her country. She worries constantly about her children, both from a moral and physical standpoint, and continually prays for their salvation. Education for the male is so important a commodity in the Woodforde household that when the third son, John, gets into trouble while at school, the incident is regarded as rather more serious than a boyish prank:

> This evening I had the cutting news that my second boy[1] was in rebellion at the College ... where he and all his Companions resolved not to make any verses, and being called to be whipped for it several of them refused to be punished, mine amongst the rest. Some of them did submit, amongst which was Cousin John Woodforde, and if the others do not, they must be expelled. God I beseech thee subdue their stubborn hearts, and give them grace to repent and accept their punishment due to their faults, and let them not run on to ruin for Christ's sake.

John later repented of his misdeeds, much to his mother's delight and relief.

Family matters were not the only ones which troubled the Woodforde household. Mary's diary covers the years when James II gained the censure of his subjects and finally expulsion from England for trying to re-Catholicize the country. The Woodforde family were staunch Protestants, yet also believed in the divine right of kings, and it was not easy for Mary to reconcile the two. But as a mother it was easy for her to see that England's troubles posed a threat to her sons, who could become soldiers and die in battle. In November 1688, Mary writes about the landing of William of Orange in England.

> Was the day as we hear the Prince of Orange landed at a place in the West. Ever since we have the sound of wars and desolation in our Land, and Soldiers continually passing up and down which keeps us in continual expectations of a Battle. But good God of all Battles do

---

[1] John was Mary's second boy but Samuel's third; Heighes's mother was Alice Beale.

thou bring good out of all our distractions and preserve our King, and establish the Church on a firm foundation. And put an end to all wars and differences between us and give peace in our days O Lord . . .

By 1689, it was clear that King James's days as King of England were over and that William and Mary would reign over England. Along with the rest of the population, Mary Woodforde welcomed the new king and queen, yet she did not forget the old King James and prayed for his welfare.

Ash Wednesday, 15, 1689. The Prince and Princess of Orange were proclaimed at London, King and Queen of England. God grant they may reign in righteousness and establish it by a firm decree, and make them a blessing to this unhappy Land. And grant us all to give to God his due, and to love him, and that true religion may flourish till the end of Time.

And good Lord bless our late King James, (wheresoever he is) with all the grace of thy holy Spirit. Open his eyes to the ways of truth, and embrace them before it is too late that tho' he has lost his earthly crown, he may obtain a Heavenly.

Mary Woodforde was a pious mother living through worried times, whose appeals to God to protect her family are reminiscent of thousands of mothers who throughout the ages have used religion as a bulwark against a troubled world.

By the time Celia Fiennes made her famous travels through England at the end of the seventeenth century, the country was all too willing to forget the political and religious struggles of the previous decades and concentrate instead on the changes which science and philosophy had brought to English life. Miss Fiennes's account of her explorations throughout the whole of England reveals a country in many ways still rural and poverty-stricken, yet changing to face the coming turmoil of the agricultural revolution of the eighteenth century.

The diaries of Celia Fiennes, originally edited in 1888 by the Hon. Mrs Emily Griffiths (as *Through England on a Side Saddle in the time of William and Mary*), reveal an extraordinarily independent woman who set out, alone for the most part, to tour England on horseback. Born in 1662, Celia came from strong Nonconformist stock. Her mother Frances was the daughter of the Roundhead Colonel Richard Whitehead and her father was Colonel Nathaniel Fiennes, the second son of William, eighth Baron and first Viscount Saye and Sele. Celia remained Nonconformist in religion and Whig in politics, and throughout her travels was always delighted when she was able to note 'here are a great many Descenters in this town'.

The main body of the journal of her travels, which lasted into the early eighteenth century, was written up from notes in 1702. The original purpose of the journeys had been to regain her health. The fact that she was able to travel alone shows the potential independence of an unmarried woman of moderate means, and suggests that the menace of the highwayman did not endanger travellers on English rural roads to the extent it did later. When Celia could, she preferred to stay with relatives or acquaintances, but when necessity dictated it she was not afraid to stay at one of the country inns along her route.

The most famous of Celia's expeditions was the 'Great Journey' of 1698 which covered northern and western England. A list of some of the cities she visited shows the magnitude of the undertaking. Starting in London she passed through Colchester, Norwich, Ely, Peterborough, Leicester, Liverpool, Kendal, Carlisle, Newcastle, Durham, Leeds, Manchester, Shrewsbury, Derby, Worcester, Gloucester, Bath, Bristol, Wells, Plymouth, Penzance, Exeter, Salisbury, Winchester and Windsor before returning to London, an undertaking to make a modern traveller wilt on the cushioned seat of his heated railway compartment. Celia's observations along the way show her to have been well aware of poverty and the less pleasant side of English country life as well as the picturesque scenery, for she was a tireless sightseer and her interests extended into unusual areas. She noted the importance of coal in Bristol, and was interested in the mining of Cornish tin. Liking new and contemporary things, she carefully noted the architecture and gardens which took her fancy, and described in detail the new formal gardens which were being laid out on English country estates.

Fearless as ever, she even passed through wild Wales during her 'Great Journey' – the principality at that time had been very little explored by English travellers. She enjoyed the scenery and the food, though one doubts if her jottings did much to enhance the image of the barbaric Welsh among the cultured English.

> From thence I went back to Harding [Hawarden] which is 8 very long miles; at Holly Well [Holywell] they speake Welsh, the inhabitants go barefoote and bare leg'd a nasty sort of people; their meate is very small here, mutton is noe bigger than little lamb, what of it there is was sweete; their wine good being neare the sea side and are well provided with fish, very good salmon and eeles and other fish I had at Harding.

Although she was impressed with the beauties of the Lake District, she was not insensitive to the terrible poverty which plagued the north of England. Like many travellers before and after her, she was appalled by the sight of people living in conditions which to her seemed to be fit only for animals. Unfortunately, like many other people with the kindest intentions, she attributed the low standard of living to the indolence and lack of purpose of the local population and failed to appreciate the true helplessness of their position.

Here I came to villages of sad little hutts made up of

drye walls, only stones piled together and the roofs of same slatt; there seemed to be little or noe tunnells for their chimneys and have no morter or plaister within or without; for the most part I tooke them at first sight for a sort of houses or barns to fodder cattle in, not thinking them to be dwelling houses, they being scattering houses here one there another, in some places there may be 20 or 30 together, and the Churches the same; it must needs be very cold dwellings but it shews something of the lazyness of the people; indeed here and there there was a house plaister'd, but there is sad entertainment . . .

Celia's interest in anything out of the ordinary and her acquisitive love of souvenirs is something very familiar to us today. From Wigan she returned with boxes made from local jet, from Cornwall she brought back souvenirs of Cornish tin, and she consumed any edible specialities of the region on the spot. Having scoured Somerset and Devon looking for a west-country tart, she finally located one in St Austins (St Austell):

. . . my Landlady brought me one of the West Country tarts, this was the first I met with, though I had asked from them in many places in Sommerset and Devonshire, its an apple pye with a custard all on the top, its the most acceptable entertainment that could be made me; they scald their creame and milk in most parts of those countrys, and so its a sort of clouted creame as we call it, with a little sugar, and soe put on the top of the apple pye; I was much pleased with my supper . . .

Although the major entries of Celia Fiennes's diaries concern her travels throughout England, when she stayed in London she studied the English system of government, writing about the processes of law and the judicial system. It is not her fault if today such weighty matters generally fail to interest readers as much as her detailed picture of

7

life outside London at the end of the seventeenth century, and her reactions to the agreeable discovery of clotted cream.

If Celia Fiennes typified the independent woman of the seventeenth century, then Fanny Burney proved that independent women could still exist within the framework of a mannered Georgian society. Her father was Dr Charles Burney, the author of a famous *History of Music* and a close friend of most of the prominent artists and writers of the time. Fanny therefore had an early exposure to a way of life where the art of conversation was rated highly, and where the visit of a celebrity like Garrick or Johnson was a commonplace. Called 'The Old Lady' by the rest of the Burney family, Fanny approached life with a dogged earnestness that pervades all her writings. Conscious always of herself and her relationships with others, Fanny Burney's diaries provide a unique view of Georgian society through the eyes of a dispassionate and acute observer.

She records one reason for her keeping a diary in one of her early journals. On 27 March 1768, she addresses a 'Certain Miss Nobody', and relishes the idea of some place where she can write down her secret thoughts without having to answer for them:

> To have some account of my thoughts, manners, acquaintance and actions when the hour arrives in which time is more nimble than memory, is the reason which induces me to keep a journal . . . I must imagine myself to be talking . . . to one whom I should take delight in confiding and remorse in concealment . . .

Between 1768 and 1783, Fanny did much more than just keep a journal. Her first novel, *Evelina*, was written secretly and published anonymously by Thomas Lowndes in 1778. It was a contemporary sensation. Fanny received just £20 for the book, a minute sum considering the popularity of the novel, and she lost a potential fortune in the royalties she never received. Her second novel, *Cecilia*, was published in 1782 and like *Evelina* was a popular success. Fanny's literary conquest was only capped by her social advancement through an acquaintance, Mrs Delaney, who lived at Windsor. Through Mrs Delaney, Fanny met King George III and Queen Charlotte. The Queen was so impressed by Fanny's manners that she offered her a post as lady-in-waiting.

This was distinctly to the advantage of the royal couple but not at all to Fanny's. Instead of her unique literary qualities finding further expression in successors to *Evelina* and *Cecilia*, her energies, mental and physical, had to be devoted to the tiresome attendance of domestic duties. As Macaulay puts it:

> ... now began a slavery of five years, of five years taken from the best part of life, and wasted in menial drudgery, under galling restraints and amidst unfriendly or uninteresting companions ...

Fanny had become a lady-in-waiting in July 1786, but soon found that the honour was not worth the discomforts of palace life. She disliked the gossip of the other ladies and found her own duties arduous and tiring. And winter in the palace was bleak, she reveals when recording a conversation with Colonel Goldsworthy, an equerry to the King.

> Diary – Queen's Lodge, Windsor, 6 Oct., 1786. But the agreeable puffs of the passages you will have just as completely as any of us. Let's see, how many blasts must you have every time you go to the Queen? First, one upon your opening your door; then another, as you get down the three steps from it, which are exposed to the wind from the garden door downstairs, then a third, as you turn the corner to enter the passage; then you come plump upon another from the hall door; then come another, fit to knock you down, as you turn to the upper passage; then, just as you turn towards the Queen's

room, comes another; and last, a whiff from the King's stairs, enough to blow you half a mile off!

In spite of the hardships, Fanny became quite intimate with many in Court circles, and her reports on the King's recurring illness and insanity show her sympathy for both the King and his wife during these difficult times. However, after five draughty years as a lady-in-waiting, Fanny found her own health was broken and she was forced to leave the palace in 1791.

Like Celia Fiennes, the Burney family believed travelling would build up Fanny's broken health, and from 1791–2 Fanny toured the western counties of England, recording all she saw. Most of these impressions are recorded in diary form in letters to her sister Susanna Elizabeth (Burney) Phillips at Mickleham. In one letter, dated Monday 8 August 1791, Fanny relates both the pleasures and discomforts for the traveller to Lyme Regis.

> The descent down to Lime is uncommonly steep; & indeed is very striking, from the magnificence of the Ocean that washes its borders. Chidiock, & Charmouth, two villages between Bridport & Lime, are the very prettiest I have ever seen.
>
> During the whole of this Post, I was fairly taken away, not only from the World, but from myself, & completly wrapt up & engrossed by the pleasures, wonders, & charms of animating Nature, thus seen in fair perfection.
>
> Lime, however, brought me to myself; for the part by the Sea, where we fixt our abode was so dirty, & *fishy*, that I rejoiced when we left it.

When Fanny had finished her wanderings, she went to visit her beloved sister who lived close to Juniper Hall, which became the refuge of a number of French aristocrats fleeing from the French Revolution. One of these unfortunates was General d'Arblay with whom Fanny very quickly fell in love. Her 'Courtship Diary' – again in the form of letters to Susanna – reveals her growing admiration and affection for the Frenchman and her desire to marry him in spite of the fact that he had lost most of his money during the Revolution.

Ignoring the disapproval of Dr Burney (he relented later, as parents are wont to do), Fanny Burney married d'Arblay on 31 July 1793 on the strength of the £100 per annum pension the Queen had given her. This sum was somewhat increased by the money Fanny made from her public writings.

In 1801, Fanny and her husband with their son Alexander went to France, where Fanny had the opportunity of reporting on the French Court circles. Her impression of Napoleon, then '*le Premier Consul*', at the Tuilleries in 1802 took the form of a diary letter addressed to Dr Burney.

As it was, I had a view so near, though so brief, of his face, as to be very much struck by it. It is of a deeply impressive cast, pale even to sallowness, while not only in the eye but in every feature – care, thought, melancholy, and meditation are strongly marked, with so much of character, nay, genius, and so penetrating a seriousness, or rather sadness, as powerfully to sink into an observer's mind.

In 1812, Fanny returned to England to nurse her father until he died. From then on the d'Arblay menage roamed through Europe. They finally settled in England after General d'Arblay retired on half-pay, having been kicked by a horse. He died in Bath in 1818 after a long illness. Fanny survived him by over twenty years, until her death in January 1840 but first having to survive another tragedy when her son Alexander died of influenza in 1837. Neither in literature nor in life was she ever to match the spectacular successes of her early years.

The most interesting of her diaries were written before her marriage to d'Arblay and describe her adventures at Court, and the people she met in the parental home.

Glimpses of such celebrities as Boswell, Johnson, Garrick and Reynolds through the young, all-seeing eyes of the opinionated yet sympathetic Miss Burney make them readily recognizable as flesh-and-blood figures rather than famous names. Her descriptions of the endless 'breakfasts' and 'calls' which were one of the few occupations of the middle-class women do much to indicate the tedium which under-lay many a genteel woman's existence. Fanny Burney's diaries are very much the product of a tightly closed society, yet they reveal a stubborn young woman who achieved what she wanted against heavy odds, and who told 'Little Miss Nobody' all the things she was unable to tell the assembled company at large.

Nancy Woodforde, a descendant of Mary Woodforde, was not as lucky as Fanny Burney. She had neither the advantages of an educated father, nor a plethora of dis-tinguished callers to while away the hours. Born in 1757, she went at the age of eighteen to live with her uncle James[1] at Weston, where she kept house for him until his death in 1803. She then went to live with her brother Samuel in London. Twenty-six of Nancy's diaries have survived and they record every detail of her daily life, though very little of the author herself. Her jottings were mostly made in such publications as 'The Suffolk Ladies Memorandum Book: or Polite Pocket Museum for the year 1793. Embellished with an elegant Engraving representing a Principal Officer receiving and introducing the Two Sons of Tippo Saib to his Excellency the Marquis Cornwallis, as Hostages. Like-wise Ten of the most fashionable Ladies Head Dresses for the Year 1793. Designed by Richter, and beautifully engraved by Audinet.'

However, it is the year 1792 which is of more interest concerning Nancy Woodforde, for in that year she kept two diaries. One was the decorated memorandum book, but it was in a more anonymous large brown notebook that

[2] James Woodforde's diary is discussed on pp. 115–20.

she revealed more about herself and her relationships with others.

In one of the first of these entries we learn about the schism between mother and daughter over her late father's estate (and, incidentally, how much a poor relation who acted as housekeeper could expect to receive).

Monday, January 9, 1792. This Day my Uncle gave me a ten Pound Bank Bill which I have every Year of him for Cloaths and Pocket Money. Thank God I have so good a Friend in him, I am sorry to say that I never have a farthing from any other of my Relations notwithstanding I have a Mother and Brothers who have plenty of Money, therefore I may say with truth I am the less obliged to them. The time will come I *hope* when I shall enjoy what my poor Father left, which is an equal share of his Estate in Sussex with my two Brothers . . .

If Nancy spends some time fretting over her lost inheritance, she also busies herself with household affairs and her own health.

Saturday, March 24, 1792. Rcd. of John Priest the following ingredients for a Diet Drink. Senna 2 oz – 8d. Sassafras 2 oz. 2d. Guiacum 6d. Jalap 1 oz 4d. Saffron ½ oz one Shilling. Rhubarb one Shilling. Maiden Hair 3d. Sweet Fennel seed 1 oz 2d. Aniseeds 1 oz 1d. Creme Tarter ½ oz 1d. . . .

(It is interesting to note how expensive saffron was – and still is – in relation to the other ingredients.)

Nancy Woodforde was fortunate in having an uncle who enjoyed her company and who took her with him when he went travelling. After one visit, to Norwich, Nancy reports on what must have been a very full day indeed, and a very pleasant one by her account.

Wednesday, May 2, 1792. Took a walk with Uncle to Mrs Brewsters and to Mr. Nosworthys where we bought a few trifles. Returned to the King's Head where I desired Mr Nosworthy to come and dress my Hair which he did and I paid him for cutting and dressing 2s. Din'd at Mr John Priests with Mrs Neal, Mrs Clarke and old Mr Priest. Mrs John Priest gave us a very handsome Dinner, fresh Salmon, Quarter of Lamb, Green Goose &c &c. After Tea Uncle and self took a Coach and went to the Theatre, which was very full indeed. Saw Hamlet and the Spoil'd Child. Mr. and Mrs. Layton there, they spoke to us and enquired for Mrs. Custance. Mr. Eaton was in our Box and chatted with us. Walk'd from the Play to the King's Head where we supped on a Lobster and went to Bed at one o Clock in the Morning.

One hopes her sweet dreams of a day well spent were not disturbed by nightmares caused by the late-night lobster. Many of the other entries in Nancy's diary concern her relationships with her neighbours and her constant complaint of the want of good company in the district. Occasionally she orders some material or has some shoes made for her, but her main social occupation is calling on the other ladies in the district. Time and time again she returns to the theme of the heartless mother who has put her in this predicament, and in a rare appeal to God she asks for justice. It is quite clear it is not her mother she misses, but the money she never receives. In this entry she reveals that she has written to her brothers concerning her father's estate.

Thursday, October 4, 1792. . . . also to desire them to consult with Mr. Messiter concerning our selling the Reversion of our Estate in Sussex, telling them that I think it would be the best thing we could do as we find our Mother has not the goodness to allow us a Single Shilling notwithstanding she has received three hundred Pounds from it since my Father died. Pray God make her a better Mother to her first born Children who have never offended her and who have been cruelly used by her.

Nancy's depression over the matter of her father's estate is heightened towards the end of the year by a visit from one Mrs Jeans and her children. Nancy feels snubbed by the fact that Mrs Jeans has not deigned to wear any fine clothes for the visit. In retaliation, Nancy wears her old ones as well. Mrs Jeans is described as a snob: 'Her Ideas are much to high for her line of Life, she talks of nothing but Drawing Rooms, Lawns and Servants, I wish she was fonder of Needlework.' When Mrs Jeans finally departs, Nancy returns to her favourite plaints on the theme of her heartless mother. However, she is not unaware of events outside the village, for she mentions the French refugees coming into England and also the sedition acts, passed ostensibly to protect the English from a revolution of their own.

Nancy Woodforde's diary of 1792 reveals a lively mind imprisoned by conventions and circumstances. Her writings suggest a woman who is delighted by lively conversation and who enjoyed a good outing as well. In spite of her difficulties with her selfish mother, who became the focus of her many frustrations, she was lucky to have an uncle who cared for her and who gave her financial protection from the vicissitudes of life which many other women had to face.

Miss Weeton's Journal of a Governess reveals the other side of the coin. These remarkable journals show what could happen to a woman who was not protected by the law and who was forced to make a life for herself on a limited income.

Miss Nelly Weeton was born on Christmas Day 1776, the daughter of a privateer who was killed not long after in an engagement with the Americans during the American War of Independence. Cheated out of her husband's spoils, Mrs Weeton, Nelly and her younger brother Tom moved to Upholland where Mrs Weeton opened a school. At the

7*

age of twenty-one, Miss Weeton lost her mother and took over the school. She made many financial sacrifices so that her brother could finish his clerkship in Leigh. She had always adored her brother and hoped that when he completed his clerkship they would be able to live together. The inevitable happened, for in 1803 Tom married a Miss Jane Scott and settled in Leigh, Lancashire. As time went on, both Tom and his wife began to look down on Miss Weeton for being a governess, and the once-happy relationship between brother and sister came to an end.

Even this break in the relationship on which she had placed so much store could not daunt Miss Weeton for long. She invested her small capital in property and left the stifling provinciality of Upholland to seek a new life in Liverpool. After an unpleasant time as a guest-companion to a Miss Chorley, she found a temporary refuge with the Winkley family and became good friends with the daughter, Miss Bessy Winkley, with whom she later corresponded. In 1809, Miss Weeton left this refuge in the interests of promotion. Opting for the extra money a new post as governess would provide, she went in this capacity to join Edward Peddar and his family for the very generous salary of 30 guineas per annum.

Her bad luck continued. Mr Peddar turned out to be an alcoholic wife-beater, and Miss Weeton's charge, his epileptic daughter, died in a fire. Miss Weeton stayed on to be a companion to his unfortunate wife, but by 1811 she had had enough, and in the grand tradition of Celia Fiennes and Fanny Burney, she travelled to soothe her shattered nerves. The journey took her to the Isle of Man, which she enjoyed both for its atmosphere and its moderate prices.

I have received a great deal of pleasure, and have not bought it dearly. £7 will include every expence of my journey, travelling, lodging, eating and servants. The hours I have spent here, have been hours of luxury indeed! Here, totally alone, my thoughts expanded with the prospect; and free and unrestrained as the air I breathed, I was happy as mortal could be.

Miss Weeton returned to the life of a governess when she accepted an engagement with Mr and Mrs Joseph Armitage at High Royd near Huddersfield in 1812. She found her new situation quite satisfactory, but she was not prepared to accept the lowly social position of the governess in such middle-class families. It was worse, she felt, than being one of the servants.

> A *Governess* is almost shut out of society; not choosing to associate with servants, and not being treated as an equal by the heads of the house or their visitors, she must possess some fortitude and strength of mind to render herself tranquil or happy; but indeed, the master or mistress of a house, if they have any goodness of heart, would take pains to prevent her feeling her inferiority. For my own part, I have not cause of just complaint; but I know some that are treated in a most mortifying manner.

Miss Weeton left this life of a governess for the supposedly more enviable life of a wife when she married Aaron Stock in 1814. But for a woman so sensible about financial and social matters, she was a terrible judge of character. Aaron Stock turned out to be a scoundrel who would take everything Miss Weeton owned including her much-beloved daughter Mary (this, moreover, with the blessing of the law, for until the Married Woman's Property Acts were passed in the late nineteenth century, married women had no right to own their own property). The crowning irony of the unfortunate marriage was that Stock's good character had been vouchsafed by her own brother Tom. He, let it be added, was the gainer by £100 under the terms of their mother's will, so he had a considerable financial interest in seeing Miss Weeton married even to the most unsuitable spouse.

After seven and a half years of ill-treatment, including

starvation and physical violence, Miss Weeton decided to leave the marital home. As the law provided no respite for ill-treated wives, Mr Stock was able to draw up a Deed of Separation with very harsh terms for his wife, including a clause allowing her to see her daughter on only three days a year, to be chosen by Mr Stock. Miss Weeton was in no position to refuse to sign such a deed, or indeed to challenge it, for she was dependent on the limited amount of money that Stock agreed to provide to enable her to exist. But her diary reveals what she really thought of such an arrangement.

> I have been just reading a Tract by Dr. Hawker – 'The Asylum for Female Penitents'. It is a beautiful and impressive piece. If paragraphs from that, and such other works, were often inserted in the Papers, I think they would do much good; and whilst so much is said in the Liverpool Mercury (and very properly) on cruelty to animals, surely Cruelty to Women is much more calling for public notice and public reproof.

Miss Weeton spent the remainder of her life travelling and trying to see her daughter. In spite of her unhappiness, her impressions on a visit to London are amusing and informative. She died in obscurity in 1844.

The diaries which Miss Weeton so carefully copied into large notebooks whenever she had the opportunity are a composite of letters and journal entries which she wished to combine into a coherent whole. Although she kept a journal for most of her life, after the birth of her child Mary she felt she had a new and greater purpose: to let the little girl know the story of her mother's past. Otherwise she thought of her jottings as self-amusement, though she may also secretly have hoped that posterity would be interested too.

> My only reasons for undertaking such a piece of work is, that it has been a great amusement during many a solitary

hour when I had no other employ, when I should only have been engaged in some fine, tedious piece of needle-work or other.

The tragedy of Miss Weeton's life is that she was never able to develop the potential of her writing. Obliged by cir-cumstances to eke out an unhappy existence as a governess in the homes of others, and, when finally married, forced to leave her husband's home and her child, she had neither the opportunity nor the inclination to write anything other than her journals. Writing was a struggle to her, yet, she herself writes, some inner compulsion perpetually kept her at it, despite what she felt was her own indolence, a feeling common to many writers.

I have long contemplated writing a History of my life, and yet have deferred it from month to month, from what must appear a very strange reason by any one who sees the quantity of my writings – the reluctance I feel to attempt writing. Whether it proceeds from indolence, or some other undefinable motive, I cannot say; but whether I have a letter to write, a journal, or an account, it seems a task to me; and yet the activity of my mind perpetually urges me to it. It is a strange contradiction, but are we not all strange contradictory beings.

Miss Weeton's journals present no startling theories on female emancipation in spite of the continual trials Miss Weeton had to endure because of her sex. Instead, in view of her own experiences, her philosophy is a very rational one:

I would not be understood to argue that woman is superior to man; I should blush to advance so weak an opinion. I would only affirm that they are *equal*, and ought to be treated as such in every respect.

Miss Weeton's tribulations make fascinating reading and provide weighty ammunition for any who would argue what an enormous difference legal measures can make to female equality.

Though the bond between Miss Weeton and her brother Tom was broken on his marriage, the love between Dorothy Wordsworth and her brother William, the poet, flourished even after William married.

Dorothy was born in Cockermouth, Cumberland, in 1791, but the early death of her parents separated her from her brothers, with whom she had been very close. Luckily, the more distant relations with whom she spent her later childhood were kind, and she was never mistreated. In 1795 her lifelong desire to live with her brother William was realized with the help of a legacy he inherited. This enabled Dorothy and William to settle in a friend's house in Racedown, Dorset. In 1797, in order to be closer to their good friend Samuel Taylor Coleridge, the Wordsworths moved to Alfoxden, near Holford in Somerset. Dorothy frequently writes of the daily walks she, William and Coleridge took on the Quantock hills. A visit to the grounds of a local squire prompts Dorothy to reflect in her Alfoxden journal of 1798 on the glories of Nature untouched.

> We walked about the squire's grounds. Quaint waterfalls about, about which Nature was very successfully striving to make beautiful what art had deformed – ruins, hermitages, etc. etc. In spite of all these things, the dell romantic and beautiful, though everywhere planted with unnaturalised trees. Happily we cannot shape the huge hills, or carve out the valleys according to our fancy.

Her journals show continually just such an extraordinary harmony with nature and people, as her simple life gently unfolded until her last tragic illness.

In December 1799, after the publication of William's *Lyrical Ballads* (in 1798) and a short stay in Germany where he worked on *The Prelude*, Dorothy and William settled in their true home in Dove Cottage in Grasmere. Dorothy loved the Lake District and the uncomplicated existence she shared with her brother. Her diaries are full of the ritual of daily life, the baking of the bread, picking of the first peas of the season, and other prosaic chores which seem to acquire a simple grandeur when Dorothy describes them. The interpolation of references to nature into the details of her domestic existence intensifies the feeling of simplicity within the greater scheme found throughout Dorothy's journals – for example, in the Grasmere journals written between 1800 and 1803:

> August 3rd, 1800. Sunday Morning. ... A Heavenly warm evening, with scattered clouds upon the hills. There was a vernal greenness upon the grass, from the rains of the morning and afternoon. Peas for dinner.

To her, vernal greenness and peas for dinner are all one in a harmonious universe.

In October 1802, Wordsworth married Mary Hutchinson after a long courtship. The introduction of another woman into the Wordsworth menage did not disturb Dorothy, and the happy two became a contented three. Even before the wedding, on an outing to Grasmere, Dorothy records in her diary her love for her sister-in-law to be. (Note that twentieth-century man is not the first creature to feel the necessity to record his name wherever he goes and that nature's greatest propagandist was not above a little vandalism.)

> We sat by the roadside at the foot of the Lake, close to Mary's dear name, which she had cut herself upon the stone. Wm cut at it with his knife to make it plainer.

Dorothy was not blinded by the beauties of the natural world. Her diaries also show her concern with the poverty and hard times which blighted the natural wonder of the Lake District, and the many beggars who came through Grasmere asking for a crust or for money make disturbing intrusions into Dorothy's secure and idyllic little world.

In literary terms, the significance of the journals Dorothy

Wordsworth kept from 1798 to 1828 extends beyond their own inherent beauty, for they provided both Wordsworth and Coleridge with inspiration for some of their most majestic poetry. The simple statements which Dorothy made about the world around her were recast as elegant and polished verse, though the sentiment remains identical. William Wordsworth's most famous poem, about the daffodils ('I wandered lonely as a cloud . . .'), came from Dorothy's impressions of the flowers as they took a lakeside walk beyond Gowbarrow Park:

> I never saw daffodils so beautiful. They grew among the mossy stones about and about them; some rested their heads upon these stones as on a pillow for weariness; and the rest tossed and reeled and danced, and seemed as if they verily laughed with the wind, that blew upon them over the lake; they looked so gay, ever glancing, ever changing.

And on a journey to London, it was Dorothy's impressions that formed the basis of another of William's masterpieces, the sonnet 'Upon Westminster Bridge'. In spite of the literary talent displayed in her diaries, Dorothy considered her own writing to be too simplistic for a poet and she was content to see her feelings and sentiments echoed in the beauties of her brother's poetry.

At the age of forty-seven, Dorothy fell ill, and she died in 1835 after a protracted illness which included some mental derangement. It is infinitely sad that so gentle a spirit could not have been given an end more fitting to the tranquillity of her life.

Caroline Fox took a more pedantic interest in literature and the literary figures of her day. She was born in 1819 in Falmouth of old Quaker stock as her name would indicate. Her father was Robert Were Fox, a shipping agent and amateur scientist – the inventor of the Dipping Needle Reflector, without which Ross the explorer claimed he would never have found the South Pole. Although Caroline met many interesting people through her father, it was rather her dwelling in Falmouth which brought her into contact with the fascinating company whose conversations fill the pages of her diary.

Falmouth and Cornwall in the mid-nineteenth century were considered good places for people with degenerative illnesses to be nursed. Among those who came to Falmouth was John Sterling, the Victorian essayist whose fame rests mainly on his writings about Carlyle. Caroline became extremely good friends with Sterling and she played a temporary Boswell to his Johnson before his early death in 1844 of a broken blood vessel. She was evidently ready for a mentor, with the essential qualification that he had to be male:

> Sterling possess a quickness and delicacy of perception quite feminine, and with it a power of originating deep and striking thoughts, and making them the foundation of a regular and compact series of consequences and deductions such as only a man, and a man of extraordinary power of close thinking and clearness of vision, can attain unto.

Deprecation of women by one with such 'clearness of vision' herself adequately suggests how women were generally regarded in Victorian days.

Caroline's circle extended to still more illustrious company, when John Stuart Mill's mother and sister arrived in Falmouth to nurse the youngest son, Henry, in a hopeless illness. Philosopher John himself arrived later, but his reputation preceded him:

> Took a walk with Clara Mill. Her eldest brother, John Stuart Mill, we understand from Sterling, is a man of extraordinary power and genius, the founder of a new school in metaphysics, and a most charming companion.

The Mills introduced her in turn to Thomas Carlyle and his wife, and she became fairly intimate with Mrs Carlyle, who led a harried existence as the wife of the dyspeptic and quarrelsome sage.

Undoubtedly, it was the company of such men as Sterling and Mill that developed the intellectual potential of Caroline Fox, and it was from their conversations that Caroline became aware of the social issues of the day and gained confidence in exploring interests of her own. In 1840, she went with the Mills to an anti-slavery meeting, where she saw Prince Albert – a 'very beautiful young man', Samuel Wilberforce, and Sir Robert Peel speak against slavery, and in 1842 she visited the Coldbath Fields Prison, where she was horrified at the treatment of women prisoners. Such medieval punishments as the treadmill were still in use, and she watched helplessly at the painful sight of the women silently walking along the hideous machine.

One of Caroline's particular interests was religion, especially the influence of the Reformation on philosophy. She believed that Catholicism was detrimental to progressive philosophy, but she was able to see the narrowness inherent in Luther's reforms. Like Mill and Sterling, and firmly in the Quaker tradition, she was concerned with the necessity of people thinking for themselves in order to free themselves from the 'trammels of authority'.

> Luther was a fine fellow, but what a moral is to be drawn from the perplexity and unhappiness of his latter days. He had taught people to *think* independently of their instructors, and had imagined that their opinions would all conform to his; when, however, they took so wide and various a scope, he was wretched, considering himself accountable for all their aberrations; and though so triumphant in his reform, shuddered at the commotion he had made, instead of viewing it as the natural and necessary result of the emancipation of thought from the trammels of authority, which he himself had introduced.

Caroline's discussions with Sterling and Dr Calvert also

covered the Italian Renaissance, with Caroline calling Savonarola a 'Roman Catholic Puritan'.

With the death of Sterling in 1844, Caroline's diaries cease to reflect the stimulus of the rigorous intellectual discussions she had with her companions. Instead they tend to be more descriptive, without the excitement of philosophical discovery. She is still an acute observer of the passing scene, and was much interested in the revolutions of 1848 and other public events such as the abdication of Louis Phillipe and his exile in England. Eventually, Caroline's own health began to fail despite the healing reputation of her own district and she travelled, like so many women diarists before her, looking without success for sun and health abroad.

Caroline Fox's fame as a diarist rests chiefly on her association with famous Victorian literary figures. She was a bright, intellectual woman, whose journals include not only records of her conversations with these eminent Victorians, but also her reactions to what they had to say. Her entries are witty and full of gaiety and her accounts of meetings with such personalities as the ageing Wordsworth, Charles Lamb, John Bright, and Tennyson delightfully revealing.

Caroline Fox was certainly no Victorian women's liberationist but her diaries provide illuminating insights into what other people thought of such matters. Her good friend John Sterling (with whom she is said to have considered marriage after his wife died) held a rather 'male chauvinist' view of the differences between the sexes, and she was for the moment content to endorse his opinions:

> Talked over the mental differences between the sexes, which he considers precisely analogous to their physical diversities, her dependence upon him – he the creative, she the receptive power.

However, five years after Sterling's death, she was introduced to Clara Balfour who gave a series of lectures on the feminine influence on history. While not completely converting Caroline to the cause, they nevertheless gave her new food for thought.

> It is curious that men expect from women a higher standard of morals and manners than they think necessary for themselves, and yet almost deny them the faculty of taking cognisance of moral questions.

In many ways, Caroline Fox was limited by the restraints which Victorian society placed upon her sex, and it was only the accident of meeting intellectual giants of her time that gave her some opportunity to develop her own potential. Unfortunately, we shall never know all she had to say, for once an edited version of her diaries had been published in 1882, her surviving sister Anna Maria burned the twelve original manuscript volumes, presumably taking the view that discretion in family affairs was more important than literary and social history.

Victoria, the Queen who gave her name to an entire era, was also an inveterate diary-keeper. She kept personal diaries, which were published in a heavily edited edition, and she also kept a journal of her experiences in Scotland which became a Victorian best-seller.

This journal, *Leaves From The Journal of Our Lives in The Highlands*, was published privately in 1867, then publicly in 1868 as one of her memorials to Albert, the Prince Consort, who had died in 1861. When the Queen was convinced that her loyal subjects might be interested in reading her diaries, she was assisted by Mr Arthur Helps, Clerk of the Privy Council, in editing the diaries and correcting the royal grammar. Mr Helps thought Her Majesty over-used the word 'so', a criticism she teased him with in their private correspondence. She could have pointed out that it was *her* English, after all!

When the volume appeared in the bookshops, it was an instant success and 20,000 copies were sold immediately. This helped the Queen out of the depression caused by the attacks on her Scottish ghillie, John Brown. Reconvinced of her popularity with the public, she contemplated a second volume, *More Leaves . . .*, which appeared in 1883. Mr Helps having died in 1875, the second work was edited by a Scottish lady, Miss Macgregor, on the guidelines set by Helps. While the first volume had been a testimonial to Albert, the second book was dedicated to John Brown, who had spent thirty-four loyal years in the Queen's service.

The Queen's reminiscences of her times in Scotland had a good deal of romantic appeal for Englishmen who knew little or nothing about the life and landscape north of the border. The novels of Sir Walter Scott and his imitators had presented Scottish traditions and nobility in a romantically favourable light and the people of England were eager to know what so fascinated their sovereign about life among the 'foreigners' of Scotland that she should spend so much time there.

Queen Victoria's first visit to Scotland in 1842 with Prince Albert (whom she had married in 1840) was a milestone in Anglo-Scottish relations. Except for a short visit by King George IV in 1822, there had been no visit to Scotland by a reigning monarch since Charles I. Even at this time, because it was one of industrial unrest provoked by the Chartist risings, the royal visit was nearly called off, and the Queen decided to visit Scotland by boat rather than to risk the roads. As if to compensate, this initial visit to Scotland was a huge success both for the Queen and in the eyes of her Scottish subjects, who lined up to cheer her wherever she and Albert appeared publicly. The Queen's account of the fisherwomen of Leith is acute and engagingly marked by Victorian propriety.

> The people were most enthusiastic, and the crowd was very great. The Porters all mounted, with curious Scotch caps, and their horses decorated with flowers, had a very singular effect; but the fishwomen are the most striking-looking people, and are generally very young and pretty women – very clean and very Dutch-looking, with their

white caps and bright-coloured petticoats. They never marry out of their class.

Victoria and Albert returned to England in love with Scotland and its people. The Queen was already subject to rheumatic pain, but her physician Sir James Clark did not hold the traditional view that Scottish weather was always wet and misty. As his son John, who was recovering from a long illness, had enjoyed good weather on the estate of Balmoral, which was at that time leased by Sir Robert Gordon, he suggested the royal couple might be equally fortunate there. Victoria and Albert accepted his recommendation and decided that their next holiday in Scotland should be taken at Deeside. Before they could return to Scotland, they heard of the sudden death of Sir Robert Gordon, and discovered that the lease on Balmoral still had twenty-seven years to run. Victoria and Albert saw sketches of the estate, remembered the medical advice, and decided to take it unseen. A holiday spent at Balmoral in 1848 confirmed their early impressions and after protracted negotiations with the Gordons, Prince Albert finally purchased Balmoral in 1852 for 30,000 guineas. Albert was much taken with the idea of improving the estate and helped to design a new palace which was built there for Victoria.

Victoria renewed her enthusiasm for the Highlands, and the times the royal family spent at Balmoral were happy ones. The very Scottish scene depicted by Victoria on the day of a fete for the members of the British Association in September 1859 suggests that they were not to be outdone by the natives:

> At two o'clock we were all ready. Albert and the boys were in their kilts, and I and the girls in royal Stewart skirts and shawls over black velvet bodices.
>
> It was a beautiful sight in spite of the frequent slight showers which at first tormented us, and the very high cold wind. There were gleams of sunshine, which, with the Highlanders in their brilliant and picturesque dresses,

the wild notes of the pipes, the band, and the beautiful background of mountains, rendered the scene wild and striking in the extreme.

Victoria and Albert did more than just spend their holidays at Balmoral. They took several 'great expeditions' touring the Scottish countryside, surveying the terrain and meeting the people who lived around their second home. The third 'great expedition' was a trip to Glen Fishie, Dalwhinnie, and Blair Athole in 1861, shortly before the Prince Consort's death. They had stopped at a small inn in Dalwhinnie. Queen Victoria comments on their disappointment at finding that an empty larder awaited them:

> ... unfortunately there was hardly anything to eat, and there was only tea, and two miserable starved Highland chickens, without any potatoes! No pudding, and no *fun*; no little maid (the two there not wishing to come in), nor our two people – who were wet and drying our and their things – to wait on us! It was not a nice supper and the evening was wet.

(If Queen Victoria thought *her* supper was poor, it was rather worse for the servants, who only had 'the remnants of our two starved chickens'.)

With the death of Prince Albert in 1861, Victoria came to rely on Balmoral more and more as a retreat from the world. Albert was constantly in her thoughts and she tried to run her life in a way she felt would be pleasing to him. In 1863, Queen Victoria was involved in an accident when her carriage turned over. Stunned, but not seriously hurt, Victoria told her companion, Princess Alice, of her still deep reliance on her dead husband.

> Almost directly after the accident happened, I said to Alice it was terrible not to be able to tell it to my dearest Albert, to which she answered: 'But he knows it all, and I am sure he watched over us'. I am thankful that

it was by no imprudence of mine, or the slightest deviation from what my beloved one and I had always been in the habit of doing, and what he sanctioned and approved.

As the Queen spent much of her widowhood in Scotland, she became more and more Scottish in outlook. On a visit to Inverlochy in 1873 (the setting for some of Bonnie Prince Charlie's wanderings in 1746 before he was able to escape back to France), she boasted of the minute quantity of Stuart blood which ran through her veins.

Yes; and *I* feel a sort of reverence in going over these scenes in this most beautiful country, which I am proud to call my own, where there was such a devoted loyalty to the family of my ancestors, – for Stewart blood is in my veins, and I am *now* their representative, and the people are as devoted and loyal to me as they were to that unhappy race.

Queen Victoria's journals of her time in Scotland do not perhaps quite merit Disraeli's clever compliment when he spoke of himself and Queen Victoria as 'we authors', but they contain accounts of many of the happier days in the life of the Queen, are amusing and informative and include some interesting sidelights on Queen Victoria's days in Scotland. The reporters who followed the royal retinue with a telescope and who became belligerent with John Brown when requested to leave the Royal Presence make a nice precedent for modern press practice.

The Queen's last visit to Balmoral was in 1900 when she was depressed by the war in South Africa and the death there of her grandson, Prince Christian Victor, of enteric fever. Her own death was but a year away. However, her two volumes of reminiscences of Scotland survive to recall the less gloomy times spent in the place she loved.

Not all women, even aristocrats, were as lucky as Queen Victoria in having the financial means to build a retreat to escape from the cares of the world. The day-to-day existence of Lady Cynthia Asquith presents a curious dichotomy between the expectations of aristocratic living and the realities of a small income.

Lady Cynthia was born in 1887, the daughter of Hugo Charteris, Lord Elcho, the 11th Earl of Wemyss (1857–1937) and Mary Wyndham. Her mother's brother was George Wyndham, who was private secretary to A. J. Balfour, and Chief Secretary for Ireland from 1900 to 1905. Cynthia was the third child in the Charteris family, having two elder brothers, Hugo and Guy, and three younger siblings, Yvo (nine years younger), Mary (eight years younger) and Irene (fifteen years younger and nicknamed 'Bibs'). The family house, Stanway, was located near Cheltenham in Gloucestershire, where the typically Victorian household coped with constantly pressing problems of finance. Among the many visitors to Stanway was Arthur Balfour, who was a close friend of Cynthia's mother.

In 1910 Lady Cynthia married Herbert Asquith, the second son of the Prime Minister, and she bore him three sons, John, Michael and Simon. Most of the Charteris family felt Cynthia's marriage to Asquith (nicknamed 'Beb' in the diaries) was unworldly because the Asquith fortune was more fiction than fact. Herbert had no country home, only an expensive town house, which had to be let for economic reasons. This left Cynthia and her babies what she called 'cuckooing' – flitting from temporary home to temporary home. 'Beb' was by profession a barrister, but he spent much of his time writing poetry. At the beginning of the First World War, he enlisted in the Royal Field Artillery.

Cynthia Asquith began her project of keeping a record of her daily life in 1915 when she was presented with a handsomely bound volume for the purpose by Duff Cooper. Her diaries are particularly interesting for three reasons. Firstly, they record the daily existence of a soldier's wife left behind during war-time (though Herbert spent a good deal of the war in England recovering from slight wounds and illnesses). Secondly, they give a good impression of the English aristocracy's reaction to the war which was to change completely their future way of life. Cynthia's own poverty makes her very aware of what other people have, and she reveals a last glimpse of a carefree and spendthrift Edwardian England. Thirdly, Lady Cynthia was herself a fascinating woman. One of the beauties of her day, painted by McEvoy, Sargent and Augustus John, she was the friend of personalities as widely differing as D. H. Lawrence and J. M. Barrie, whose secretary she became for many years. Her reflections on the company she kept and the changing society she lived in present a fascinating picture of England during the First World War.

In 1915, the implications of the war had not yet made an impact on the doyens of 'high society'. While 'Beb' was in training at Littlehampton, Lady Cynthia could still afford to be wry about the multitudes who also flocked to the seaside.

> Monday, 5th July, 1915. . . . We went down to the beach, but the wind made it intolerable and we returned to the pleasant shelter of our garden. Such a ghastly population in the hotel. I told Beb they represented England and were what he was really fighting for, and he nearly resigned his commission.

For the most part, the war seemed a mere extension of the playing fields of Eton, an enormous game, where the possibility of death added a touch of excitement to the rules. At this early stage few were yet aware of the full horrors of war and the impact it was to have on civilian life. In 1915, Lady Cynthia notes in her diary a Zeppelin raid over London and how it seemed more like an evening of fireworks than a German attack on the heart of London.

> Mamma and Bibs had just arrived from Scotland, and we dined with them, Letty (Lady Violet Manners, 2nd daughter of the 8th Duke of Rutland and wife of Hugo,

Cynthia's eldest brother) and Mary at Queen's Restaurant, Sloane Square. Just as we had finished, and were emerging, there was a bustle and we heard the magic word 'Zeppelin'. We rushed out and found people in dramatic groups, gazing skywards. Some men there said they saw the Zeppelin. Alas, I didn't! But our guns were popping away and shells bursting in the air. I felt excited pleasurably, but not the faintest tremor and I longed and longed for more to happen. Bibs was the only member of the family who had sufficient imagination to be frightened and Letty's fun was spoilt by the thought of the children. My only words were: 'Something for my diary!'

The reality of the war came all too soon to touch Lady Cynthia's life. Her youngest brother Yvo died in 1915 and Letty's husband Hugo was to die in 1916. Many of her friends were to die in battle including two men with whom she had had flirtations. Lord Basil Blackwood, on whom she had come to depend so much as a friend and companion, joined the Grenadier Guards and was killed in 1917 (he was also a friend of Hilaire Belloc's, and illustrator of Belloc's *Bad Child's Book of Beasts*), and Lord Alexander Thynne, brother of the Fifth Marquess of Bath and a major in the Royal Wilts. Yeomanry, was tragically killed at the end of the war in 1918. Thus fell the shadow of death on a large number of middle- and upper-class young men who had gaily volunteered for battle, only to lose their illusions and their lives in a few months of modern warfare.

Thursday, 11th November, 1915. Oh why was I born for this time? Before one is thirty to know more dead than living people? Stanway, Clouds [the Wyndham country home in Wiltshire], Gosford [principal seat of the Earl of Wemyss near Edinburgh] – all the settings of one's life – given up to ghosts. Really, one hardly knows who is alive and who is dead. One thing is that now at least people will no longer bury their dead as they used. Now they are so many one *must* talk of them naturally and humanly, not banish them by only alluding to them as if it were almost indelicate.

Cynthia did not give in to the depression of the war. She did some hospital work, but also carried on her social life with practically as much vigour as before the war. Luncheons, dinners, visits to the theatre and shopping expeditions occupied her time much as they had done formerly. Smart, intelligent and witty conversations were imbued with as much importance as they were in the days of Fanny Burney or Caroline Fox, and Lady Cynthia was fortunate to know many of the people who were making news at the time. Through her marriage to Herbert, she had a great deal to do with the Asquiths, particularly the Prime Minister's wife, Margot, who was never at a loss for a witty or audacious comment.

D. H. Lawrence evidently thought a great deal of Lady Cynthia's opinions, for he sent her copies of his novels to read before the publication day. She had the literary acuteness to be impressed by his work, but like many of his critics at the time, disliked the bluntness of his physical description.

> I read the whole of Lawrence's last novel, *The Rainbow*, which he had sent me. A strange bewildering, disturbing book. It is full of his obsessions about sex conflict (all the lovers hate one another) and the 'amorphousness' of actual life. Excellent bits of writing, but still too much over-emphasis and brutality. One cannot count how often and how gratuitously he employs the word 'belly'.

It may seem from a casual glance at her diaries that Lady Cynthia was a careless mother who spent little time with her children between social engagements. It is true that her two sons John and Michael (Simon was born in 1919) were often boarded out to willing relatives, but it was a family misfortune which really spoiled her happiness with her children. John was an autistic child, and because so little was then known about autism that it could not be correctly diagnosed, Lady Cynthia was depressed and confused about the behaviour of her child. Though periodic visits to different doctors and governesses gave her occasional cause to hope, she was only to be plunged into depression again later. In an attempt to bring the family together, Lady Cynthia rented an inexpensive apartment in London, where her experiences with the telephone company suggest that nothing changes:

> Maddening morning. Was disconnected from the telephone owing to the previous tenant not having paid her bill. All my expostulations with the controller were in vain – they refused to reconnect me until they received the cheque. It was just like having one's tongue cut out.

One interesting facet of Cynthia Asquith's diary is her realization of how the war changed her. There are constant references to the almost surreal quality of life that took over as death became commonplace and living lost its dignity. In October 1918, on the verge of a nervous breakdown, Cynthia Asquith tries to reason out the coming armistice.

> I am beginning to rub my eyes at the prospect of peace. I think it will require more courage than anything that has gone before. It isn't until one leaves off spinning around that one realises how giddy one is. One will have to look at long vistas again, instead of short ones, and one will at last fully recognise that the dead are not only dead for the duration of the war.

The diaries of Lady Cynthia Asquith are those of a woman of leisure, yet her sensitivity to the problems engendered by the First World War echo the feelings of many women living in England at that time.

For Katherine Mansfield, born in New Zealand in 1888, the same war was to bring the death of a beloved brother. At the age of fourteen, Katherine had come to London where she entered Queen's College in Harley Street. In 1906, she returned to New Zealand, but she soon wished to come back to England. After two years, with the help of a modest allowance from her father, she was able to return to London. In 1909, she married George Bowden, a man she did not know very well, and she left him the day after the wedding. Katherine found she was pregnant, and her mother arranged for her to stay at a Bavarian convent. Here she had a miscarriage, but was later able to use her experiences in Germany as the basis of some of her best short stories.

Katherine formed a more satisfactory emotional relationship with John Middleton Murry, whom she met in 1911. They lived together from April 1912 until 1918 when Katherine was able to secure a divorce from her first husband. She and Murry were married in May 1918. With Murry, in spite of rather straitened circumstances, Katherine was able to concentrate on her writing. Although ill-health dogged her all her life, she wrote constantly and with versatility, producing short stories, reminiscences and reviews. Her first collection of short stories appeared in 1911 and during the pre-war years she contributed to *The New Age*, *Rhythm*, and *The Blue Review*, of which Murry was associate editor.

The coming of the First World War coincided with a decline in Katherine's health. The combination of nervous strain, pleurisy and the death of her brother Leslie Heron Beauchamp in 1915 caused her tremendous anguish:

> *Brother.* I think I have known for a long time that life was over for me, but I never realised it or acknowledged it until my brother died. Yes, though he is lying in the middle of a little wood in France and I am still walking upright and feeling the sun and the wind from the sea, I am just as much dead as he is. The present and the future mean nothing to me. I am no longer 'curious' about people; I do not wish to go anywhere; and the only

possible value that anything can have for me is that it should put me in mind of something that happened or was when we were alive.

She became absorbed by her childhood memories of New Zealand, using them to produce *Prelude* (1918) and *Je ne parle pas français*, which was privately printed in 1919.

In 1917, Katherine Mansfield was found to be consumptive and she began long travels all over Europe in an attempt to regain her health. In 1919, John Middleton Murry became editor of the *Athenaeum*, for which Katherine reviewed novels. Husband and wife were frequently apart during Katherine's last years, as she tried to find some refuge from the distressing symptoms of her disease. In September 1919, she went to San Remo where she took a furnished cottage, the 'Casetta'. For a time her spirits improved.

> Death, December 15, 1919. When I had gone to bed I realised what it was that had caused me to 'give way'. It was the effort of being up, with a heart that wouldn't work. Not my lungs at all. [Katherine always believed she would die of heart failure rather than consumption.] My despair simply disappeared – yes, *simply*. The weather was lovely. Every morning the sun came in and drew those squares of golden light on the wall, I looked round my bed on to a sky like silk. The day opened slowly, slowly like a flower, and it held the sun long, long before it slowly folded. Then my homesickness went. I not only didn't want to be in England, I began to love Italy, and the thought of it – the sun – even when it was too hot – always the sun – and a kind of wholeness which was good to bask in.

However, her condition worsened.

> January 8, 1920. BLACK. A day spent in Hell. Unable to do anything. Determined not to weep – wept. Sense of isolation frightful. I shall die if I don't escape.

Nauseated, faint, cold with misery. Oh, I *must* survive it somehow . . .

Despite her deteriorating health, Katherine Mansfield still managed to publish more of her stories. Among the editions which appeared after the war and before her death were *Bliss* (1920) which established her as a major writer, and *The Garden Party* (1922), the last book to be published before her death.

Discouraged by her failure to throw off the tuberculosis, she grasped at the straw of a spiritual cure when medicine failed to give her the ease she craved. In a vain attempt to compose her spiritual life she entered the Gurdjieff Institute near Fontainebleau in October 1922. However, the spartan life of the Institute was designed for hardier physiques than that of the waning Katherine and she died of a pulmonary haemorrhage on 9 January 1923.

Katherine Mansfield's diary is the painful revelation of a dying woman still trying to achieve perfection in her writing. While her physical condition and the fragility of her constitution were themselves pitiful, her intense search for artistic satisfaction brought her another kind of pain. In 1914, even before her health had begun seriously to deteriorate, she suffers mental anguish when her writing does not reach her own high standards.

> I have begun to sleep badly again and I've decided to tear up everything that I've written and start again. I'm sure that is best. This misery persists, and I am so crushed under it. If I could write with my old fluency for *one day*, the spell would be broken. It's the continual effort – the slow build-up of my idea and then, before my eyes and out of my power, its slow dissolving.

In 1920, in spite of her continual bad health, Katherine Mansfield's search for perfection and for purity (to lead her to her spiritual cure) in order to become 'worthy' of good writing, is still her major concern, even as death looms before her.

I haven't been able to yield to the kind of contemplation that is necessary. I have not felt pure in heart, not humble, not good. There's been a stirring-up of sediment. I look at the mountains and I see nothing but mountains.

The appearance of Katherine Mansfield's diary in this chapter, rather than in that on writers' diaries may seem strange. But her extraordinary ability to rise above the life of an invalid, to dedicate herself absolutely to her writing and to make a success of herself in a predominantly man's world, is as much the triumph of the woman as the writer.

The last woman diarist in this chapter had the benefit of a childhood in France: Marie Belloc Lowndes, only daughter of a French father and an English mother, and sister of Hilaire Belloc. Her father died in her early childhood, and she spent the rest of her childhood and adolescence in France and England, finally settling permanently in London.

In 1909 Marie married an Englishman, F. A. Lowndes, who was on the staff of *The Times* until his retirement in 1938. He died in 1940. Through her husband's and her own connections, she knew many of the major political and literary figures of her time, including George Meredith, Oscar Wilde, the Asquiths and H. G. Wells. In her own right Mrs Lowndes became a well-known writer, having over fifty books to her credit by the time of her death. One of her most famous books was *The Lodger* (1913), which was one of the first psychological murder stories. The diaries which she kept from 1911 to 1947 (the year of her death) are interesting from the woman's, the writer's and the general observer's viewpoint.

The pre-First World War years in England saw a great deal of change in the status of women. For the first time women were able to go out and earn their own living without being considered a blight on their family's name. Occupations which were formerly considered only hobbies for well-off women could be approached with the dedication which men brought to similar jobs. Writing was one occupation in which women began to exert a new spirit of professionalism and to command respect for their endeavours. At a meeting of the Women Writers' Dinner Committee, Mrs Lowndes took part in a discussion on professional ethics. The question was whether the writer of an evidently scandalous book entitled *Letters From a Flapper at the Durbar* should be asked to dinner. One distinguished woman writer refused to attend the dinner if the young girl were asked and Mrs Lowndes upheld her for these reasons.

> I upheld her on the point that any woman who has disgraced herself professionally should not be asked by us. What a person does in private life seems to me to be none of our business; this was proved by the fact that we are asking half a dozen women who have been very notorious in the last year; but I do not think we ought to ask a novelist who writes pornographic work or a journalist who does work against the whole feeling of what is decent in the profession.

While Mrs Lowndes upheld the professional ethics of writers, she was also aware of the inequality of women in the larger sphere of society. It was still a man's world, particularly in the prosperous middle classes, where youth and beauty in women were considered more important than intelligence or development of character.

> We all talked about the enduring power of love. Some of those present said that love goes in a man when the woman becomes middle-aged. I said that it often amazed me to see how love endured though I admitted that in a certain class – the prosperous commercial class, no man, whatever his age, has any use for a woman, even for her company, after she is, say, forty. That is one of the things that strikes me in one circle I frequent. The moment you know a man at all well, he confides to you

quite frankly what a bore he finds his wife's friends – that being a man of sixty talking of women between forty and forty-five.

During the First World War, less tragic for Mrs Lowndes than for Lady Cynthia Asquith, she followed the political activity and military campaigns avidly, but she was also greatly saddened by the effect on ordinary people of the political situation.

April 10th, 1917. There has been a spate of very early marriages and I heard of a lady who was asked if she was happy about her youthful son's marriage. She replied 'I don't know what I should feel if it were not wartime, for in that case he would still be at Harrow!'

Mrs Lowndes was a realistic and sensible woman. Like Katherine Mansfield, she was not content with the literary quality of all her books, but she did not suffer Katherine Mansfield's continual remorse. Instead, her comments on her own writings reflect her well-integrated life and ability to make the most of the talents she possessed.

March 9th, 1923. On the other hand the fact, of which I was long ignorant, that I possess hidden away what is called a 'plot mind' became of very great importance to me as a writer. A plot mind, is curiously rare, and does secure for its owner a kind of immortality. By that I mean that long after the writer is dead, the books go on being reprinted.

During the inter-war years, Mrs Lowndes's diaries are full of the interesting topics of the time. She writes very completely about the abdication of Edward VIII and is most sympathetically disposed to Mrs Simpson. She seems also to have made good use of all her political and literary connections to find out the details of the topics in which she was interested. With the coming of the Second World War, she declared herself to be firmly anti-appeasement, and was astute regarding Hitler's future plans. Her French practicality comes to the surface when she reveals her own personal preparations for the coming of the war.

> September 29, 1938. I was guided by my experience in the last war. The fact that I had a gross of matches in the early August of 1914 was of the greatest value. It is one of the things – strange to say – in which there quickly becomes a shortage. I also found then the great value of rice when cooked and mixed with fried onions and a little butter: it really makes a meal for anyone. I ran out of methylated in the last war and had great trouble making my early morning tea before my work – in fact, I was forced to use the Tommy Cookers and the stuff people used for heating their hair tongs, both expensive and unpleasant to use.

With her perceptive comments on social and political affairs, her common-sense approach to problems within her profession and her domestic circumstances, Mrs Lowndes gives some indication of how far women had progressed since the days of Mary Woodforde, the seventeenth-century diarist with whom this chapter began. In the past, women keeping diaries had been the exceptions, yet their diaries show that despite the social plight of women, the human qualities of wit, perception and sensitivity had to find an outlet. That the qualities were shown in the boudoir rather than the drawing-room and demonstrated only in the privacy of a journal has been society's loss but unquestionably the diary's gain.

BIBLIOGRAPHY

Mary Woodforde's diary in *Woodforde Papers and Diaries*, edited and with an introduction by Dorothy Heighes Woodforde (Peter Davies, 1932).

The Journeys of Celia Fiennes, edited and with an introduction by Christopher Morris, foreword by G. M. Trevelyan (The Cresset Press, 1949).

Fanny Burney: *Diary*, first published 1842 and 1846. Many editions since, including *Fanny Burney's Diary*, A Selection from the Diary and Letters, edited by John Wain (The Folio Society, London, 1961).

Nancy Woodforde's diary in *Woodforde Papers and Diaries*, edited and with an introduction by Dorothy Heighes Woodforde (Peter Davies, 1932).

Miss Weeton's Journal of a Governess, a reprint of *Miss Weeton: Journal of a Governess*, vol. 1 1807–1811, vol. 2 1811–1825, vol. 1 – new introduction by J. J. Bagley, vol. 2 – revised epilogue by Edward Hall (David and Charles, 1969).

Dorothy Wordsworth: *Journals*, edited by W. Knight in 2 volumes (Macmillan, 1897) and a number of later editions.

Memories of Old Friends Being Extracts From the Journals and Letters of Caroline Fox, from 1835–1871, vol. 1 and vol. 2 (Smith, Elder and Co., 1882).

Victoria in the Highlands, the personal journal of Her Majesty Queen Victoria with notes, introductions, and a description of the acquisition and rebuilding of Balmoral Castle, by David Duff (Frederick Muller, 1968).

Lady Cynthia Asquith: *Diaries 1915–1918*, with a foreword by L. P. Hartley (Hutchinson, 1968).

Journal of Katherine Mansfield, edited by John Middleton Murry (Definitive Edition, Constable, 1954).

Diaries and Letters of Marie Belloc Lowndes 1911–1947, edited by Susan Lowndes (Chatto & Windus, 1971).

ELEVEN

The Diary in Modern Life

As an epilogue to this survey of some of the outstanding British diaries of the past – and I stress that the survey is strictly personal and claims neither to be comprehensive nor definitively representative – it is perhaps worth considering what the term 'diary' has come to mean in modern parlance. If the average man in the street, always supposing that there were such a creature, were asked if he keeps a diary, then his probable immediate reaction would be to extract a small pocket-sized notebook, perhaps with a pencil in the spine, from the inner recesses of his jacket. He probably does not think in terms of a daily book of memoirs, reminiscence or self-analysis; he thinks of a memory aid which enables him not to forget that his mother-in-law is coming next Tuesday, and that he really ought not to delay planting bulbs any longer than the following Friday.

The firm responsible for about half the market for the modern diary – which involves producing nearly ten million diaries a year – is Charles Letts and Company Limited. A little research into their history has revealed some interesting facts about the diary, and confirmation of some of the trends revealed elsewhere in this book.

For example, I have in front of me a Letts pocket diary for 1974. Some of the Letts 1974 diaries reflect the fact that this is very much the 1970s: one has Common Market holidays and the days of the week in French, German and Italian, unthinkable even a few years ago. The pocket diary, though, is worth examination not so much for its modern features – metrification information, world populations and time variations from Greenwich Mean Time – but for what it retains from the past. We are still nominally a Christian country, though every poll taken on the subject reveals that the percentage of the population for whom the Christian pattern of life has much significance is beoming smaller and smaller. This is in complete contrast to the Middle Ages when the Christian religion completely dominated daily life. Even in the nineteenth century, life revolved around the Church to a great extent. The Letts pocket diary reminds us of this past tradition, for although Epiphany, Advent, Ash Wednesday and the like may now be of interest to very few, they retain their place in the modern diary. (I am excepting those Christian holidays which have become secular feasts – Christmas Day, etc.) In fact, an attempt made by Letts to tidy up one of their diaries for 1973 by omitting ecclesiastical information drew a protest from the Mothers' Union.

The pocket diary also omits, as many do not, tide tables. One might wonder what the relevance of tide tables is to the un-nautical mind of the average diary buyer. Very little, it has to be admitted, and the only reason for their presence in many modern diaries is that they were always included in days gone by. They were included, of course, because they were once of vital importance to city merchants awaiting the arrival of ships to fix prices, buy supplies and generally to direct the course of their commercial life; and, because no one has thought it worthwhile to take the tide tables out, there they remain, a small vestige of history in a modern product.

The history of the firm of Letts has another significance in the story of the diaries of the past. Its original founder was John Letts, a relatively untutored youth who was born in the heart of the City of London in the parish of St Peter's Church, Cornhill, in 1772. At the end of a long life (he was seventy-nine when he died) and despite a retirement spent at Broxbourne, Hertfordshire, he was buried in a vault at St Peter's, a few streets away from his birthplace and from his place of work. As soon as his limited schooling was over, he was apprenticed to a master bookbinder. Somehow, after his years of apprenticeship had ceased, he accumulated enough from his wages to set up in 1809 an establishment of his own as a stationer (a fact borne out by the Post Office Directory of the day, which then listed occupations as well as addresses) at 95 Royal Exchange. He was thirty-seven at the time. The economic climate was not particularly auspicious for new ventures, for the bulk of John Letts' customers must have been the merchant bankers and members of the shipping companies dealing with the hazards of business during a spate of European Wars.

From about 1816 onwards he operated as both stationer and printer, and one of his products was a '*Letts' Diary* or *Bills Due and Almanack*', a bound volume which provided space for day-by-day accounting of transactions. Joined in the business by his son Thomas, John Letts, who became known to his clients as 'Honest Jack', must have continued to prosper, for by 1836 he was producing no less than twenty-eight different diary formats and designs. Between the years 1816 and 1836 were two significant dates in the history of the diary – the publication of John Evelyn's diary in 1818 and the publication of Samuel Pepys's diary in 1825.

In other words, Honest Jack was supplying a new product, a commercially-produced diary, at just the time that diary-keeping was in the news and when people may have felt keen to emulate their distinguished predecessors. Moreover, in visiting the small bow-fronted premises of Letts at the Royal Exchange, the new customers were leaving their coffee houses and going where Pepys had gone a century and a half before them to see the king, Charles II, 'lay the first stone of the first pillar of the new building of the Exchange'. (The original exchange had been destroyed in the Great Fire of 1666, and, ironically enough, the second was similarly destroyed in 1838.)

Thomas Letts was probably a far more astute business-man than his one-time apprentice father. (There is some evidence that relations between them were far from smooth, which may well reflect a conflict between the older, more conservative man and his impatient and go-ahead son.) He rode the disruption of the second Royal Exchange fire from temporary premises in Cornhill, he diversified his activities so that the firm, now called Letts Son and Co., were described as 'Printers, Map and Chart Sellers and Pocket Book Manufacturers', and he continued to expand the diary side of the business. In 1872 he took advantage of the changes in company law made in the 1850s and 1860s to claim limited liability, further evidence of his business acumen, for the conversion of old businesses to limited liability companies was generally slow before about 1880. Within the diary itself, he added a preface to convince customers of the desirability of the product, arguing the merits of the diary over the family Bible for the important family records of the past, and continued:

So much for events of the *Past* and *Present*; but it is the *Future* we regard with most favour for our protégé. It should, if properly kept, be the means of distinctly indicating, either through *specific entry* for that purpose, or experience derived from the study of registered facts, *when it would be advisable to do, or to provide for, what is necessary or desirable to have done, to enquire into, or to look out for*. Matters these of equally frequent occurrence with the *thrifty housewife*, the *man of business*, of *science*, and of *pleasure*. *All* of us occasionally require to be reminded of (and if not, sometimes, to our grief, forget) what we would gladly and certainly have effected with timely notice. By adopting this course, we have a Perpetual Monitor, at once unerring and faithful, and yet withal neither intrusive nor costly. Nay! should any of our readers be economically disposed, he may adopt this volume as his *One* Diary for Life, and so save *annual* purchase of the wherin [*sic*] it may have been his practice to invest.

To such as can afford the additional outlay, we strongly recommend the adoption of Russia binding, and a spring lock with duplicate keys; for while the former lasts for ever and looks handsome, the latter keeps back the impertinent eye of idle curiosity.

As a piece of mid-Victorian salesmanship this could hardly be bettered, and it is apparent that the reasons for the success of the diary suggested by Thomas Letts over a century ago still hold good. What, save 'Perpetual Monitors' are they, after all?

By the 1870s, Thomas had relinquished his active engagement with the firm in favour of his sons, perhaps remembering the reluctance his own father had shown in handing over. However, in obtaining the necessary finance for the expansion of the business, the Letts family had to relinquish to some extent their exclusive control of the company. In fact, it is probable that Thomas's sons, the managers Thomas Alton Letts, and particularly Charles Letts, were chafing at the knowledge that the real power of decision-making lay elsewhere. The diary of Charles's first wife, begun in 1869 and continued by Charles himself after her death, is full of small grumbles about the follies of company business, the appointment of new men of whom Charles disapproved, and so on. Unfortunately, the diary breaks off in 1879, denying us a first-hand account of the dramatic events of 1881 when the final split between the Letts family and the constituted company took place.

Whatever the motives and emotions now obscured by the passing of a hundred years, there can be no doubt that Charles then took a bold if not almost foolhardy step. With £500 of his own, and another £700 which he borrowed, he set up a small business of his own at the Royal Exchange where his grandfather had started it all. He was already forty-five, with four children to support, and his staff amounted to one traveller, one order clerk, one apprentice and one warehouseman. Running on credit and enthusiasm, he called himself 'Printer in American Type' and subsequently 'Printer'. The old firm of Letts Son and Co. Ltd, retaining the name of Letts but without a member of the Letts family, struggled on a few more years, but was wound up and liquidated in 1885.

One of their creditors was probably Cassell and Co., the distinguished directory and book publishers, for Cassell's from about 1890 onwards were calling themselves 'Publishers of the original Letts Diaries'. Later they must have decided to concentrate on what they could do best, and forsook diary publishing, but it is interesting that Honest Jack's invention made it worthwhile to continue with the name of Letts as if the family name and the diary were to be thought of as one.

Charles, meanwhile, was not having the easiest of times. His first six months brought him a modest profit of £67, his first full year lost him £355, and it was not until the end of the 1880s that he began to show a profit. He brought his two sons into the business, Harry in 1888 and Norman in 1895. It would seem that the profitability of his business was ultimately dependent on the diary, for it was the expansion of the diary side of the venture which moved in parallel with his later financial success. As early as 1884 he was producing a part-work publication, *A Hundred Best Pictures*, an imaginative and aesthetic achievement, but probably, alas, rather too early for the public to appreciate it. A catalogue of his products which survives is titled 'Pens, Ink and Paper By C.L.' Only at the back of the catalogue, after pages describing various papers, envelopes and inks, are diaries mentioned. The existence of the other firm causes him to phrase things carefully:

CHARLES LETTS'S DIARIES
These diaries are compiled
by Mr. Charles Letts – *the only*
Letts now in the Diary Trade
– and for many years Editor
of the Original Series . . .

For what is evidently only a small section of his business, he offers a comprehensive range. There are twenty-one kinds of cloth-bound diaries, thirty-nine kinds of scribbling diaries, and fourteen kinds of cheap, cloth-bound diaries. And as if that were not enough, he appears to have been the father of the range of special interest diaries we know today with his list of 'Special Diaries'.

Charles Letts's Ideal Medical Visiting List – Got up in the most modern style, and forms a comprehensive pocket companion for the Medical practicioner. Includes pages for Obstetric and Vaccination Engagements, Engagements under the Factory Act, Patients' and Nurses' Addresses, Monthly Cash Account, Accounts asked for, Memo, of things Wanted, Memo. of Loans, and important Memoranda. Leatherette, with Flap and Pencil, 56 visits, 2s. 6d. 112 visits, 3s. 6d.; French Morocco Tuck, or Flap and Band, 56 Visits, 3s. 6d.; 112 visits, 4s. 6d.

The Church Kalendar – Contains table of lessons, ecclesiastical colors for the various seasons, with brief ritual directions gathered from the office books of the Ancient English Church, short notices of Saints, and tables of duration of moonlight for every day in the year. Sheet form, printed in red and black, or book form, with blank pages for memoranda, 1s.

In addition to these and other similar diaries, he produced special notebooks such as *Charles Letts's Pew Rent Register*, *Charles Letts's Farmers' Labourers Accounts Book*, and *Charles Letts's Wine Bin Book*: here is the beginning of an enterprise no less remarkable than that of Honest Jack – providing specialist diaries for specialist interests. By 1900, the firm was selling nearly a quarter of a million diaries. By 1909, when Charles took his well-earned retirement, this had almost tripled. Despite a dip in sales caused by the First World War, by about 1936 they had soared to three million. There was another decrease in sales during the Second

World War, but in 1945 the firm completed some ticklish negotiations with Hazell Watson and Viney, to whom had passed the right once held by Cassell's to use the name Letts. Consequently, a new generation of the Letts family was able to take over the firm knowing that they had an exclusive right to use the family name and an opportunity to sell Letts diaries all over the world. By 1949 sales had reached four million; they now stand at just under ten million. With a young generation of Letts in charge, the commercial future of the Letts diary for desk and pockets would seem to be ensured. What, however, will be the fate of the diary as a literary form? Has it turned full circle and reverted to the impersonal pre-seventeenth-century engagement book? Will mass communication and the widespread dissemination of information take away the urge of man to record the events of his day?

Certainly, there is some danger of this happening. However, as long as there are egos which crave audiences beyond their immediate contemporaries, and as long as man retains sufficient individuality to believe that he is not exactly as other men are, it is unlikely the time will come when there are no diarists. If anyone reading these words has found an answering chord from any of the numerous diarists whose work we have been discussing, then I hope that he or she will put down this book, pick up a pen, and write, 'Dear Diary . . .'